Kama Sutra

Kama Sutra

The Perfect Bedside Companion

BLACK DOG
& LEVENTHAL
PUBLISHERS
NEW YORK

Published by
Black Dog & Leventhal Publishers, Inc.
151 West 19th Street
New York, NY 10011

Distributed by
Workman Publishing Company
708 Broadway
New York, NY 10003

Manufactured in China

Cover and interior design by Sheila Hart Design
All artwork courtesy of The Bridgeman Art Library International
except page 19 courtesy PhotoDisc and
pages 25 and 123 courtesy of Victoria & Albert Museum, London/Art Resource, NY

ISBN: 1-57912-280-9

h g f e

Adapted from *The Kama Sutra of Vatsyayana* translated by Sir Richard Burton.

Library of Congress Cataloging-in-Publication Data available on file.

CONTENTS

SOCIETY AND SOCIAL CONCEPTS

On the Acquisition
of Dharma, Artha, and Kama

an, the period of whose life is one hundred years, should practice Dharma, Artha, and Kama at different times and in such a manner that they may harmonize, and not clash in any way. He should acquire learning in his childhood; in his youth and middle age he should attend to Artha and Kama; and in his old age he should perform Dharma, and thus seek to gain Moksha, that is, release from further transmigration. Or, because of the uncertainty of life, he may practice them at times when they

On the Acquisition of Dharma, Artha, and Kama

are enjoined to be practiced. But one thing is to be noted: he should lead the life of a religious student until he finishes his education.

Dharma is obedience to the command of the Shastra, or Holy Writ, of the Hindus to do certain things, such as the performance of sacrifices, which are not generally done because they do not belong to this world, and produce no visible effect; and not do other things, such as eating meat, which is often done because it belongs to this world, and has visible effects.

Dharma should be learned from the Shruti (Holy Writ), and from those conversant with it.

Artha is the acquisition of arts, land, gold, cattle, wealth, equipages, and friends. It is also the protection of

what is acquired, and the increase of what is protected.

Artha should be learned from the king's officers, and from merchants who may be versed in the ways of commerce.

Kama is the enjoyment of appropriate objects by the five senses of hearing, feeling, seeing, tasting, and smelling, assisted by the mind together with the soul. The ingredient in this is a peculiar contact between the organ of sense and its object, and the consciousness of pleasure that arises from that contact is called Kama.

Kama is to be learned from the *Kama Sutra* (aphorisms on love) and the practice of citizens.

When all three, Dharma, Artha, and Kama, come together, the former is better than the one which follows it; that is, Dharma is better than Artha, and Artha is better than Kama. But Artha should always be first practiced by the king, for the livelihood of men is to be obtained from it only. Again, Kama being the occupation of public women, they should prefer it to the other two, and these are exceptions to the general rule.

Objection

Some learned men say that as Dharma is connected with things not belonging to this world, it is appropriately treated of in a book; and so also is Artha, because it is practiced only by the application of proper means, and a knowledge of those means can be obtained only by study and from books. But Kama being a thing which is practiced even by the brute creation, and which is to be found everywhere, does not want any work on the subject.

Answer

This is not so. Sexual intercourse, being a thing dependent on man and woman, requires the application of proper means by them, and those means are to be learned from the *Kama Shastra*. The nonapplication of proper means, which we see in the brute creation, is caused by their being unrestrained, and by the females among them being fit for sexual intercourse at certain seasons only and no more, and by their intercourse not being preceded by thought of any kind.

Objection

The Lokayatikas[1] say: Religious ordinances should not be observed, for they bear a future fruit, and at the same time it is also doubtful whether they will bear any fruit at all. What foolish person will give away that which is in his own hands into the hands of another? Moreover, it is better to have a pigeon today than a peacock tomorrow; and a copper coin we have the certainty of obtaining is better than a gold coin the possession of which is doubtful.

Answer

It is not so. First, Holy Writ, which ordains the practice of Dharma, does not admit of a doubt.

Second, sacrifices such as those made for the destruction of enemies, or for the fall of rain, are seen to bear fruit.

Third, the sun, moon, stars, planets, and other heavenly bodies appear to work intentionally for the good of the world.

Fourth, the existence of this world is

1 These were certainly materialists who seemed to think that a bird in the hand was worth two in the bush.

On the Acquisition of Dharma, Artha, and Kama

affected by the observance of the rules respecting the four classes[2] of men and their four stages of life.

Fifth, we see that seed is thrown into the ground with the hope of future crops.

Vatsyayana is therefore of the opinion that the ordinances of religion must be obeyed.

Objection

Those who believe that destiny is the prime mover of all things say: We should not exert ourselves to acquire wealth, for sometimes it is not acquired although we strive to get it, while at other times it comes to us itself without any exertion on our part. Everything is therefore in the power of destiny, who is the lord of gain and loss, of success and defeat, of pleasure and pain.

Thus we see that Bali[3] was raised to the throne of Indra by destiny, and was also put down by the same power, and only destiny can reinstate him.

Answer

It is not right to say so. As the acquisition of every object presupposes at all events some exertion on the part of man, the application of proper means may be said to be the cause of gaining all our ends, and this application of proper means being thus necessary (even where a thing is destined to happen), it follows that a person who does nothing will enjoy no happiness.

Objection

Those who are inclined to think that Artha is the chief object to be obtained argue thus: Pleasures should not be sought for, because they are obstacles to the practice of Dharma and Artha,

Among the Hindus the four classes of men are the Brahmans, or priestly class; the Kshatriyas, or warrior class; the Vaishya, or agricultural and mercantile class; and the Shudra, or menial class. The four stages of life are: the life of a religious student (Brahmacarin), the life of the householder (Grihastha), the life of a Vanaprastha, or forest dweller, and the life of a Sannyasin, or wandering ascetic.
Bali was a demon who had conquered Indra and gained his throne, but was afterward overcome by Vishnu at the time of his fifth incarnation.

On the Acquisition of Dharma, Artha, and Kama

which are both superior to them, and are also disliked by meritorious persons. Pleasures also bring a man into distress, and into contact with low persons; they cause him to commit unrighteous deeds, and produce impurity in him; they make him regardless of the future, and encourage carelessness and levity. And, lastly, they cause him to be disbelieved by all, received by none, and despised by everybody, including himself. It is notorious, moreover, that many men who have given themselves up to pleasure alone have been ruined along with their families and relations. Thus King Dandakya[4] of the Bhoja dynasty, carried off a Brahman's daughter with

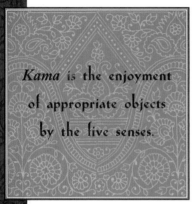

Kama is the enjoyment of appropriate objects by the five senses.

4 Dandakya is said to have abducted from the forest the daughter of a Brahman, named Bhargava, and being cursed by the Brahman, was buried with his kingdom under a shower of dust. The place was called after his name the Dandaka Forest, celebrated in the *Ramayana* but now unknown.

Man, the period of whose life is one hundred years, should practice Dharma, Artha, and Kama at different times and in such a manner that they may harmonize, and not clash in any way.

evil intent, and was eventually ruined and lost his kingdom. Indra, too, having violated the chastity of Ahalya,[5] was made to suffer for it. In like manner the mighty Kichaka,[6] who tried to seduce Draupadi; and Ravana,[7] who attempted to gain over Sita, were punished for their crimes. These and many others fell by reason of their pleasures.

Answer

This objection cannot be sustained, for pleasures, being as necessary for the existence and well-being of the body as food, are consequently equally required. They are, moreover, the results of Dharma and Artha. Pleasures are, therefore, to be followed with moderation and caution. No one refrains from cooking food because there are beggars to ask for it, or from sowing seed because there are deer to destroy the corn when it has grown up.

5 Ahalya was the wife of the sage Gautama. Indra caused her to believe that he was Gautama, and thus enjoyed her. He was cursed by Gautama and subsequently afflicted with a thousand ulcers on his body.

6 Kichaka was the brother-in-law of King Virata, with whom the Pandavas had taken refuge for one year. Kichaka was killed by Bhima, who assumed the disguise of Draupadi. For this story the *Mahabharata* should be referred to.

7 The story of Ravana is told in the *Ramayana*; the *Ramayana* and the *Mahabharata* are the two great epic poems of the Hindus; the latter was written by Vyasa, and the former by Vlamiki.

Thus a man practicing Dharma, Artha, and Kama enjoys happiness both in this world and in the world to come. The good perform those actions in which there is no fear as to what is to result from them in the next world, and in which there is no danger to their welfare. Any action which conduces to the practice of Dharma, Artha, and Kama together, or of any two, or even of one of them, should be performed, but an action which conduces to the practice of one of them at the expense of the remaining two should not be performed.

On the Acquisition of Dharma, Artha, and Kama

On the Arts and Sciences to Be Studied

an should study the *Kama Sutra* and the arts and sciences subordinate thereto, in addition to the study of the arts and sciences contained in Dharma and Artha. Even young maids should study this *Kama Sutra*, along with its arts and sciences, before marriage, and after it they should continue to do so with the consent of their husbands.

Here some learned men object, and say that females, not being allowed to study any science, should not study the *Kama Sutra*.

On the Arts and Sciences to Be Studied

But Vatsyayana is of opinion that this objection does not hold good, for women already know the practice of *Kama Sutra*, and that practice is derived from the *Kama Shastra*, or the science of Kama itself. Moreover, it is not only in this but in many other cases that, though the practice of a science is known to all, only a few persons are acquainted with the rules and laws on which the science us based. Thus the Yajnikas, or sacrificers, though ignorant of grammar, make use of appropriate words when addressing the different deities, and do not know how these words are framed. Again, persons do the duties required of them on auspicious days, which are fixed by astrology, though they are not acquainted with the science of astrology. In a like manner riders of horses and elephants train these animals

Even young maids should study this *Kama Sutra* along with its arts and sciences, before marriage, and after it they should continue to do so with the consent of their husbands.

without knowing the science of training animals, but from practice only. And similarly the people of the most distant provinces obey the laws of the kingdom from practice, and because there is a king over them, and without further reason.[1] And from experience we find that some women, such as the daughters of princes and their ministers, and public women, are actually versed in the *Kama Shastra*.

> A female should learn the *Kama Shastra*... by studying its practice from some confidential friend.

A female, therefore, should learn the *Kama Shastra*, or at least a part of it, by studying its practice from some confidential friend. She should study alone, in private, the sixty-four practices that form a part of the *Kama Shastra*. Her teacher should be one of the following persons; namely, the daughter of a nurse brought up with her and already married,[2] or a female friend who can be trusted in everything, or the sister of her mother (that is, her aunt), or an old female servant, or a female beggar who may have formerly lived in the family, or her own sister, who can always be trusted.

The following are the arts to be studied, together with the *Kama Sutra*:

1 Singing.

2 Playing on musical instruments.

3 Dancing.

4 Union of dancing, singing, and playing instrumental music.

1 The author wishes to prove that a great many things are done by people from practice and custom, without their being acquainted with the reason of things, or the laws on which they are based, and this is perfectly true.

2 The proviso of being married applies to all the teachers.

5   Writing and drawing.

6   Tattooing.

7   Arraying and adorning an idol with rice and flowers.

8   Spreading and arranging beds or couches of flowers, or flowers upon the ground.

9   Coloring the teeth, garments, hair, nails, and bodies, that is, staining, dyeing, coloring, and painting them.

10   Fixing stained glass into a floor.

11   The art of making beds, and spreading carpets and cushions for reclining.

12   Playing on musical glasses filled with water.

13 Storing and accumulating water in aqueducts, cisterns, and reservoirs.

14 Picture making, trimming, and decorating.

15 Stringing of rosaries, necklaces, garlands, and wreaths.

16 Binding of turbans and chaplets, and making crests and topknots of flowers.

17 Scenic representations. Stage playing.

18 Art of making ear ornaments.

19 Art of preparing perfumes and odors.

20 Proper disposition of jewels and decorations, and adornment in dress.

21 Magic or sorcery.

On the Arts and Sciences to Be Studied

22 Quickness and dexterity in manual skill.

23 Culinary art, that is, cooking and cookery.

24 Making lemonades, sherbets, acidulated drinks, and spirituous extracts with proper flavor and color.

25 Tailor's work and sewing.

26 Making parrots, flowers, tufts, tassels, bunches, bosses, knobs, and so on, out of yarn or thread.

27 Solution of riddles, enigmas, covert speeches, verbal puzzles, and enigmatical questions.

28 A game which consists in repeating verses, and as one person finishes, another person has to commence at once, repeating another verse, beginning

Her teacher should
be one of the
following persons
namely, the daughter
of a nurse brought
up with her or
a female friend
who can be trusted
in everything

with the same letter with which the last speaker's verse ended. Whoever fails to repeat, is considered to have lost and to be subject to pay a forfeit or stake of some kind.

29 The art of mimicry or imitation.

30 Reading, including chanting and intoning.

31 Study of sentences difficult to pronounce. It is played as a game, chiefly by women and children, and consists of a difficult sentence being given; and when it is repeated quickly, the words are often transposed or badly pronounced.

32 Practice with a sword, single-stick, quarterstaff, and bow and arrow.

33 Drawing inferences, reasoning or
    inferring.

34 Carpentry, or the work of a carpenter.

35 Architecture, or the art of building.

36 Knowledge about gold and silver
    coins, and jewels and gems.

37 Chemistry and mineralogy.

38 Coloring jewels, gems, and beads.

39 Knowledge of mines and quarries.

40 Gardening; knowledge of treating the
    diseases of trees and plants, of nourish-
    ing them, and determining their ages.

41 Arts of cockfighting, quail fighting,
    and ram fighting.

42 Art of teaching parrots and starlings to speak.

43 Art of applying perfumed ointments to the body, and of dressing the hair with unguents and perfumes, and braiding it.

44 The art of understanding writing in cipher and the writing of words in a peculiar way.

45 The art of speaking by changing the forms of words. It is of various kinds. Some speak by changing the beginning and end of words, others by adding unnecessary letters between every syllable of a word, and so on.

46 Knowledge of languages and of the vernacular dialects.

47 Art of making flower carriages.

48 Art of framing mystical diagrams, of addressing spells and charms, and binding armlets.

49 Mental exercises, such as completing stanzas or verses on receiving a part of them; or supplying one, two, or three lines when the remaining lines are given indiscriminately from different verses, so as to make the whole an entire verse with regard to its meaning; or arranging the words of a verse written irregularly by separating the vowels from the consonants, or leaving them out altogether; or putting into verse or prose sentences represented by signs or symbols. There are many other such exercises.

50 Composing poems.

51 Knowledge of dictionaries and vocabularies.

On the Arts and Sciences to be Studied

52 Knowledge of ways of changing and disguising the appearance of persons.

53 Knowledge of the art of changing the appearance of things, such as making cotton to appear as silk, coarse and common things to appear as fine and good.

54 Various ways of gambling.

55 Art of obtaining possession of the property of others by means of mantras or incantations.

56 Skill in youthful sports.

57 Knowledge of the rules of society, and of how to pay respects and compliments to others.

58 Knowledge of the art of war, of arms, armies, and so on.

59 Knowledge of gymnastics.

60 Art of knowing the character of a man from his features.

61 Knowledge of scanning or constructing verses.

62 Arithmetical recreations.

63 Making artificial flowers.

64 Making figures and images in clay.

A public woman, endowed with a good disposition, beauty, and other winning qualities, and also versed in the above arts, obtains the name of a Ganika, or public woman of high quality, and receives a seat of honor in an assemblage of men. She is, moreover, always respected by the king, and praised by learned men,

The daughter of a king, too, as well as the daughter of a minister, being learned in the above arts, can make their husbands favorable to them.

and her favor being sought for by all, she becomes an object of universal regard. The daughter of a king, too, as well as the daughter of a minister, being learned in the above arts, can make their husbands favorable to them, even though these may have thousands of other wives besides themselves.

And in the same manner, if a wife becomes separated from her husband, and falls into distress, she can support herself easily, even in a foreign country, by means of her knowledge of these arts. Even the bare knowledge of them gives attractiveness to a woman, though the practice of them may be possible only according to the circumstances of

A man who is versed in these arts... gains very soon the hearts of women.

each case. A man who is versed in these arts, who is loquacious and acquainted with the arts of gallantry, gains very soon the hearts of women, even though he is acquainted with them for only a short time.

On the Arts and Sciences to Be Studied

The Life of the Citizen[1]

aving thus acquired learning, a man, with the wealth that he may have gained by gift, conquest, purchase, deposit,[2] or inheritance from his ancestors, should become a house-holder (Grihastha), and pass the life of a citizen. He should take a house in a city or large village, or in the vicinity of good men, or in a place which is the resort of many persons. This abode should be situated near some water, and divided into different compartments for different purposes. It should be surrounded by a garden, and also con-

1 This term would appear to apply generally to an inhabitant of Hindustan. It is not meant only for a dweller in a city, like the Latin Urbanus as opposed to Rusticus.

2 Gift is peculiar to a Brahman, conquest to a Kshatriya, while purchase, deposit, and other means of acquiring wealth belong to the Vaishya.

The Life of the Citizen

tain two rooms, an outer and an inner one. The inner room should be occupied by the females, while the outer room, balmy with rich perfumes, should contain a bed, soft agreeable to the sight, covered with a clean white cloth, low in the middle part, having garlands and bunches of flowers[3] upon it, and a canopy above it, and two pillows, one at the top, another at the bottom. There should be also a sort of couch, and at the head of this a sort of stool, on which should be placed the fragrant ointments for the night, such as flowers, pots containing collyrium and other fragrant substances, things used for perfuming the mouth, and the bark of the common citron tree.

> This abode should be divided into different compartments for different purposes.

3 Natural garden flowers.

The outer room,
balmy with rich
perfumes, should
contain a bed, soft
agreeable to the sight,
covered with a
clean white cloth
...and a canopy
above it.

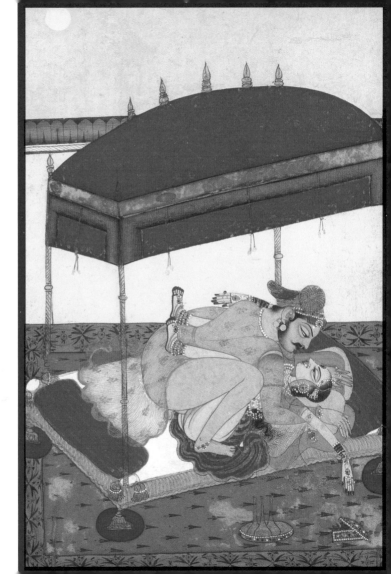

Near the couch, on the ground, there should be a pot for spitting, a box containing ornaments, and also a lute hanging from a peg made of the tooth of an elephant, a board for drawing, a pot containing perfume, some books, and some garlands of the yellow amaranth flowers. Not far from the couch, and on the ground, there should be a round seat, a toy cart, and a board for playing with dice; outside the outer room there should be cages of birds,[4] and a separate place for spinning, carving and suchlike diversions. In the garden there should be a whirling swing and a common swing, as well as a bower of creepers covered with flowers, in which a raised parterre should be made for sitting.

Now, the householder, having got up in the morning and performed his necessary duties,[5] should wash his teeth, apply a limited quantity of ointments and perfumes to his body, put some ornaments on his person and collyrium on his eyelids and below his eyes, color his lips with alacktaka,[6] and look at himself in the glass. Having then eaten betel leaves, with other things that give fragrance to the mouth, he should perform his usual business. He should bathe daily, anoint his body with oil every other day, apply a lathering[7] substance to his body every three days, get his head (including face) shaved every four days, and the other parts of his body every five or ten days.[8] All these things should be done without fail, and the sweat of the armpits should also be removed. Meals should be taken in the forenoon, in the afternoon, and again at night, according to Charayana. After breakfast, parrots

[4] Such as quails, partridges, parrots, starlings, etc.

[5] The calls of nature are always performed by the Hindus the first thing in the morning.

[6] A color made from lac.

[7] This would act instead of soap, which was not introduced until the rule of the Muslims.

[8] Ten days are allowed when the hair is taken out with a pair of pincers.

and other birds should be taught to speak, and the fighting of cocks, quails, and rams should follow. A limited time should be devoted to diversions with Pithamardas, Vitas, and Vidushakas,[9] and then the midday sleep should be taken.[10] After this, the householder, having put on his clothes and ornaments, should, during the afternoon, converse with his friends. In the evening there should be singing, and after that the house holder, along with his friend, should await in his room, previously decorated and perfumed, the arrival of the woman that may be attached to him, or he may send a female messenger for her or go to her himself. After her arrival at his house, he and his friends should welcome her and entertain her with a loving and agreeable conversation. Thus end the duties of the day.

9 These are characters generally introduced in the Hindu drama; their characteristics will be explained further on.

10 Noonday sleep is allowed only in summer, when the nights are short.

11 These are very common in all parts of India.

12 In the *Asiatic Miscellany*, and in Sir William Jones's works, will be found a spirited hymn addressed to this goddess who is adored as the patroness of the fine arts, especially of music and rhetoric, as the inventress of the Sanskrit language, etc. She is the goddess of harmony, eloquence, and language, and is somewhat analogous to Minerva. For further information about her see Edward Moor's *The Hindoo Pantheon*.

The following are the things to be
done occasionally as diversions or
amusements:

1 Holding festival[11] in honor of different deities.

2 Social gatherings of both sexes

3 Drinking parties

4 Picnics

5 Other social diversions

Festivals

On some particularly auspicious day,
an assembly of citizens should be
convened in the temple of Saraswati.[12]
There are the skill of singers, and of
others who may have come recently
to the town, should be tested, and on
the following day they should always

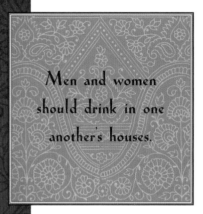

Men and women should drink in one another's houses.

be given some rewards. After that, they may either be retained or dismissed, according as their performances are liked or not by the assembly. The members of the assembly should act in concert both in times of distress as well as in times of prosperity, and it is also the duty of these citizens to show hospitality to strangers who may have come to the assembly. What is said above should be understood to apply to all the other festivals which may be held in honor of the different deities according to the present rules.

Social Gatherings

When men of the same age, disposition, and talents, fond of the same

13 The public women, or courtesans (Vesya), of the early Hindus have often been compared with the Hetera of the Greeks. The subject is dealt with at some length in H. H Wilson's *Select Specimen of the Theatre of the Hindoos*, in two volumes (Trübner and Co., 1871 It may be fairly considered that the courtesan was one of the elements and an important element too, of early Hindu society and that her education and intellect were both superior to that of the

diversions and with the same degree of education, sit together in company with public women,[13] or in an assembly of citizens, or at the abode of one among themselves, and engage in agreeable discourse with each other, such is called sitting in company or a social gathering. The subjects of discourse are to be the completion of verses half composed by others, and the testing of the knowledge of one another in the various arts. The women who may be the most beautiful, who may like the same things that the men like, and who may have the power to attract the minds of others, are here done homage to.

Drinking Parties

Men and women should drink in one another's houses. And here the men should cause the public women to drink, and should then drink them-

women of the household. Wilson says: "By the Vesya or courtesan, however, we are not to understand a female who has disregarded the obligation of law or the precepts of virtue, but a character reared by a state of manners unfriendly to the admission of wedded females into society, and opening it only at the expense of reputation to women who were trained for association with men by personal and mental acquirements to which the matron was a stranger."

selves, liquors such as the Madhu, Aireya, Sura, and Asawa, which are of bitter and sour taste; also drinks concocted from the barks of various trees, wild fruits, and leaves.

Going to Gardens or Picnics

In the forenoon, men, having dressed themselves, should go to gardens on horseback, accompanied by public women and followed by servants. And having done there all the diversions, such as the fighting of quails, cocks, and rams, and other spectacles, they should return home in the afternoon in the same manner, bringing with them bunches of flowers, and so on.

The same also applies to bathing in summer in water from which poisonous or dangerous animals have previously been taken out, and which has been built in on all sides.

The Life of the Citizen

Other Social Diversions

Spending nights playing with dice. Going out on moonlight nights. Keeping the festive day in honor of spring. Plucking the sprouts and fruits of the mango trees. Eating the fibers of lotuses. Eating the tender ears of corn. Picniking in the forests when the trees get their new foliage. The Udakakshvedika, or sporting in the water. Decorating each other with the flowers of some trees. Pelting each other with the flowers of the Kadamba tree, and many other sports which may either be known to the whole country or may be peculiar to particular parts of it. These and similar amusements should always be carried on by citizens.

The above amusements should be followed by a person who diverts himself alone in company with a courtesan, as well as by a courtesan who can do the same in company with her maidservants or with citizens.

A Pithamarda[14] is a man without wealth, alone in the world, whose only property consists of his Mallika,[15] some lathering substance, and a red cloth, who comes from a good country, and who is skilled in all the arts; and by teaching these arts is received in the company of citizens, and in the abode of public women.

A Vita[16] is a man who has enjoyed the pleasures of fortune, who is a compatriot of the citizens with whom he associates, who is possessed of the

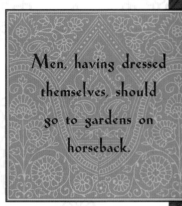

Men, having dressed themselves, should go to gardens on horseback.

[14] According to this description a Pithamarda would be a sort of professor of all the arts, and as such received as the friend and confidant of the citizens.

[15] A seat in the form of the letter *T*.

[16] The Vita is supposed to represent somewhat the character of the Parasite of the Greek comedy. It is possible that he was retained about the person of the wealthy, and employed as a kind of private instructor, as well as an entertaining companion.

qualities of a householder, who has his wife with him, and who is honored in the assembly of citizens and in the abodes of public women, and lives on their means and on them.

A Vidushaka[17] (also called a Vaihasaka, that is, one who provokes laughter) is a person acquainted with only some of the arts, who is a jester, and who is trusted by all.

These persons are employed in matters of quarrels and reconciliations between citizens and public women. This remark applies also to female beggars, to women with their heads shaven, to adulterous women, and to old public women skilled in all the various arts.

Thus a citizen living in his town or village, respected by all, should call on

17 Vidushaka is evidently the buffoon and jester. Wilson says of him that he is the humble companion, not the servant, of a prince or man of rank, and it is a curious peculiarity that he is always a Brahman. He bears more affinity to Sancho Panza, perhaps, than any other character in Western fiction, imitating him in his combination of shrewdness and simplicity, his fondness of good living and his love of ease. In the

the persons of his own caste who may be worth knowing. He should converse in company and gratify his friends by his society; and obliging others by his assistance in various matters, he should cause them to assist one another in the same way.

There are some verses on this subject, as follows:

"A citizen discoursing, not entirely in the Sanskrit language[18] nor wholly in the dialects of the country, on various topics in society, obtains great respect. The wise should not resort to a society disliked by the public, governed by no rules, and intent on the destruction of others. But a learned man living in a society which acts according to the wishes of the people and which has pleasure for its only object is highly respected in this world."

dramas of intrigue he exhibits some of the talents of Mercury, but with less activity and ingenuity, and occasionally suffers by his interference. According to the technical definition of his attributes he is to excite mirth by being ridiculous in person, age, and attire.

18 This means, it is presumed, that the citizen should be acquainted with several languages. The middle part was perhaps a reference to the Thugs.

ON SEXUAL UNION

Kinds of Union According to Dimensions, Force of Desire or Passion, and Time

an is divided into three classes: the hare man, the bull man, and the horse man, according to the size of his lingam.

Woman also, according to the depth of her yoni is either a female deer, a mare, or a female elephant.

There are thus three equal unions between persons of corresponding dimensions, and there are six unequal unions when the dimensions do not correspond, or nine in all, as the following table shows:

Kinds of Union According to Dimensions,
Force of Desire or Passion, and Time

EQUAL

Men	Women
Hare	Deer
Bull	Mare
Horse	Elephant

UNEQUAL

Men	Women
Hare	Mare
Hare	Elephant
Bull	Deer
Bull	Elephant
Horse	Deer
Horse	Mare

There are, then,
nine kinds of
union according
to dimensions.
Among all these,
equal unions
are the best.

In these unequal unions, when the male exceeds the female in point of size, his union with a woman who is immediately next to him in size is

called high union, and is of two kinds; while his union with the woman most remote from him in size is called the highest union, and is of one kind only. On the other hand, when the female exceeds the male in point of size, her union with a man immediately next to her in size is called low union, and is of two kinds; while her union with a man most remote from her in size is called the lowest union, and is of one kind only.

In other words, the horse and mare, the bull and deer, form the high union, while the horse and deer form the highest union. On the female side, the elephant and bull, the mare and hare, form low unions, while the elephant and the hare make the lowest unions.

There are, then, nine kinds of union according to dimensions. Among all these, equal unions are the best; those of a superlative degree, that is, the highest and the lowest, are the worst, and the rest are middling, and with them the high[1] are better than the low.

There are also nine kinds of union according to the force of passion or carnal desire, as follows:

Men	Women
Small	Small
Middling	Middling
Intense	Intense

High unions are said to be better than low ones, for in the former it is possible for the male to satisfy his own passion without injuring the female, while in the latter it is difficult for the female to be satisfied by any means.

Kinds of Union According to Dimensions, Force of Desire or Passion, and Time

Men	Women
Small	Middling
Small	Intense
Middling	Small
Middling	Intense
Intense	Small
Intense	Middling

A man is called a man of small passion whose desire at the time of sexual union is not great, whose semen is scanty, and who cannot bear the warm embraces of the female.

Those who differ from this temperament are called men of middling passion, while those of intense passion are full of desire.

In the same way, women are supposed

to have the three degrees of feeling as specified above.

Lastly, according to time there are three kinds of men and women: the short-times, the moderate-timed, and the long-timed, and of these, as in the previous statements, there are nine kinds of union.

But on this last head there is a difference of opinion about the female, which should be stated.

Auddalika says: "Females do not emit as males do. The males simply remove their desire, while the females, from their consciousness of desire, feel a certain kind of pleasure, which gives them satisfaction, but it is impossible for them to tell you what kind of pleasure they feel. The fact from which this becomes evident is that

Kinds of Union According to Dimensions,
Force of Desire or Passion, and Time

males, when engaged in coition, cease of themselves after emission, and are satisfied, but it is not so with females."

This opinion is, however, objected to on the grounds, that if a male be long-timed, the female loves him the more, but if he be short-timed she is dissatisfied with him. And this circumstance, some say, would prove that the female emits also.

But this opinion does not hold good, for if it takes a long time to allay a woman's desire, and during this time she is enjoying great pleasure, it is quite natural then that she should wish for its continuation. And on this subject there is a verse as follows:

"By union with men the lust, desire, or passion of women is satisfied, and the pleasure derived from the consciousness of it is called their satisfaction."

The followers of Babhravya, however, say that the semen of women continues to fall from the beginning of the sexual union to its end; and it is right that it should be so, for if they had no semen there would be no embryo.

> "By union with men the lust, desire, or passion of women is satisfied."

To this there is an objection. In the beginning of coition the passion of the woman is middling, and she cannot bear the vigorous thrusts of her lover; but by degrees her passion increases until she ceases to think about her body, and then finally she wishes to stop from further coition.

This objection, however, does not hold good, for even in ordinary things that revolve with great force, such as a potter's wheel or a top, we find that the motion at first is slow, but by degrees it becomes very rapid. In the same way the passion of the woman having gradually increased, she has a desire to discontinue coition, when all the semen has fallen away. And there is a verse with regard to this as follows:

"The fall of the semen of the man takes place only at the end of coition, while the semen of the woman falls continually; and after the semen of both has all fallen away then they wish for the discontinuance of coition."

Lastly, Vatsyayana is of opinion that the semen of the female falls in the same way as that of the male.

In the beginning of coition the passion of the woman is middling... but by degrees her passion increases until she ceases to think about her body.

Now, someone may ask here: If men and women are beings of the same kind, and are engaged in bringing about the same result, why should they have different work to do?

Vatsyayana says that this is so because the ways of working, as well as the consciousness of pleasure in men and women, are different. The difference in the ways of working, by which men are actors and women are the persons acted upon, is owing to the nature of the male and female; otherwise the actor would be sometimes the person acted upon, and vice versa. And from this difference in the ways of working follows the difference in the consciousness of pleasure, for a

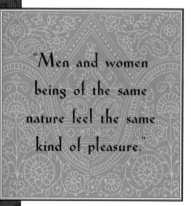

"Men and women being of the same nature feel the same kind of pleasure."

This is a long dissertation very common among Sanskrit authors, both when writing and talking socially. They start certain propositions, and then argue for and against them. What is presumed the author means is that, though both men and women derive pleasure from the act of coition, the way it is produced is brought about by different means, each individual performing his own work in the matter irrespective of the other, and each deriving individually his own consciousness of pleasure from the act performed. There is a difference in the work that each does, and a difference in the consciousness of pleasure that each has, but no difference in the pleasure they feel, for each feels that pleasure to a greater or lesser degree.

man thinks, "This woman is united with me," and a woman thinks, "I am united with this man."

It may be said that if the ways of working in men and women are different, why should there not be a difference, even in the pleasure they feel, which is the result of those ways?

But this objection is groundless, for the person acting and the person acted upon being of different kinds, there is a reason for the difference in their ways of working; but there is no reason for any difference in the pleasure they feel, because they both naturally derive pleasure from the act they perform.[2]

On this again some may say that when different persons are engaged in doing the same work, we find that they accomplish the same end or purpose;

Kinds of Union According to Dimensions, Force of Desire or Passion, and Time

while, on the contrary, in the case of men and women we find that each of them accomplishes his or her own end separately, and this is inconsistent. But this is a mistake, for we find that sometimes two things are done at the same time; as for instance in the fighting of rams, both the rams receive the shock at the same time on their heads. Or in throwing one wood apple against another, or in a fight or struggle of wrestlers. If it be said that in these cases the things employed are of the same kind, it is answered that even in the case of men and women, the nature of the two persons is the same. And as the difference in their ways of working arises from the difference of their conformation only, it follows that men experience the same kind of pleasure as women do. There is also a verse on this subject as follows:

"Men and women being of the same nature feel the same kind of pleasure, and therefore a man should marry such a woman as will love him ever afterward."

The pleasure of men and women being thus proved to be of the same kind, it follows that in regard to time there are nine kinds of sexual intercourse, in the same way as there are nine kinds according to the force of passion.

There being thus nine kinds of union with regard to dimensions, force of passion, and time, respectively, by making combinations of them innumerable kinds of union would be produced. Therefore in each particular kind of sexual union, men should use such means as they may think suitable for the occasion.

Kinds of Union According to Dimensions, Force of Desire or Passion, and Time

At the first time of sexual union the passion of the male is intense, and his time is short, but in subsequent unions on the same day the reverse of this is the case. With the female, however, it is the contrary, for at the first time her passion is weak, and her time long, but on subsequent occasions on the same day her passion is intense and her time short, until her passion is satisfied.

On the Different Kinds of Love

Men learned in the humanities are of opinion that love is of four kinds:

1 Love acquired by continual habit

2 Love resulting from the imagination

3 Love resulting from belief

4 Love resulting from the perception of external objects

1   Love resulting from the constant and
continual performance of some act is
called love acquired by constant practice and habit; as for instance, the
love of sexual intercourse, the love of
hunting, the love of drinking, the love
of gambling, and so on.

2   Love which is felt for
things to which we are
not habituated, and
which proceeds entirely
from ideas, is called love
resulting from imagina-
tion; as for instance, that
love which some men
and women and eunuchs
feel for the Auparishtaka,
or mouth congress, and
that which is felt by all

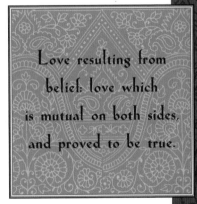

Love resulting from
belief: love which
is mutual on both sides,
and proved to be true.

for such things as embracing, kissing,
and so on.

3   The love which is mutual on both sides, and proved to be true, when each looks upon the other as his or her very own; such is called love resulting from belief by the learned.

4   The love resulting from the perception of external objects is quite evident and well known to the world, because the pleasure it affords is superior to the pleasure of the other kinds of love, which exist only for its sake.

What has been said in this chapter upon the subject of sexual union is sufficient for the learned; but for the edification of the ignorant, the same will now be treated at length and in detail.

Kinds of Union According to Dimensions, Force of Desire or Passion, and Time

ON THE EMBRACE

his part of the *Kama Shastra*, which treats of sexual union, is also called "Sixty-four" (Chatushshashti). Some old authors say that it is called so because it contains some sixty-four chapters. Others are of opinion that the author of this part being a person named Panchala, and the person who recited the part of the Rig-Veda called "Dashtapa," which contains sixty-four verses, being also called Panchala, the name "Sixty-four" has been given to the part of the work in honor of the Rig-Veda. The followers

On the Embrace

of Badhravya say on the other hand that this part contains eight subjects: the embrace, kissing, scratching with the nails or fingers, biting, lying down, making various sounds, playing the part of a man, and the Auraparishataka, or mouth congress. Each of these subjects being of eight kinds, and eight multiplied by eight being sixty-four, this part is therefore named "Sixty-four." But Vatsyayana affirms that as this part contains also the following subjects, namely striking, crying, the acts of a man during congress, the various kinds of congress, and other subjects, the name "Sixty-four" is given to it only accidentally. As for instance, we say this tree is "Saptaparna," or seven-leaved; this

> This part of the *Kama Shastra,* which treats of sexual union, is also called "sixty four" (Chatushshashti).

When two lovers...
rub their bodies
against each other,
it is called a
"rubbing embrace."

offering of rice is "Panchavarna," or five-colored; but the tree has not seven leaves, nor does the rice five colors.

However, the part "Sixty-four" is now treated of; and the embrace, being the first subject, will now be considered.

The embrace which indicated
the mutual love of a man and woman
who have come together
is of four kinds:

> Touching
>
> Piercing
>
> Rubbing
>
> Pressing

The action in each case is denoted by the meaning of the word which stands for it.

1   When a man under some pretext or other goes in front of or alongside a woman and touches her body with his own, it is called the "touching embrace."

2   When a woman in a lonely place bends down, as if to pick something up, and pierces, as it were, a man sitting or standing, with her breasts, and the man in return takes hold of them, it is called a "piercing embrace."

> The embrace which indicated the mutual love... is of four kinds: Touching, Piercing, Rubbing, Pressing.

These two embraces take place only between persons who do not, as yet, speak freely with each other.

3   When two lovers are walking slowly together, either in the dark or in a place of public resort, or in a lonely

place, and rub their bodies against each other, it is called a "rubbing embrace."

4   When on the above occasion one of them presses the other's body forcibly against a wall or pillar, it is called a "pressing embrace."

These two last embraces are peculiar to those who know the intentions of each other.

At the times of meeting, the four following kinds of embrace are used:

Jataveshtitaka, or the twining of a creeper.

Vrikshadhirudhaka, or climbing of a tree.

Tila-Tandulaka, or the mixture of sesame seed with rice.

Kshiraniraka, or milk-and-water
embrace.

1   When a woman, clinging to a man as
a creeper twines round a tree, bends
his head down to hers with the desire
of kissing him and slightly makes
the sound of *Sūt, sūt*, embraces him,
and looks lovingly toward him, it is
called an embrace like the "twining
of a creeper."

2   When a woman, having
placed one of the feet
on the foot of her lover,
and the other on one of
his thighs, passes one of
her arms round his
back, and the other on
his shoulders, makes
slightly the sounds of
singing and cooing, and
wishes, as it were, to

> When lovers lie on a
> bed, and embrace...
> this is called an
> embrace like
> "the mixture of sesame
> seed with rice."

On the Embrace

climb up on him in order to have a kiss, it is called an embrace like the "climbing of a tree."

3   These two embraces take place when the lover is standing.

When lovers lie on a bed, and embrace each other so closely that the arms and thighs of one are encircled by the arms and thighs of the other, and are, as it were rubbing up against them, this is called an embrace like "the mixture of sesame seed with rice."

4   When a man and a woman are very much in love with each other, and, not thinking of any pain or hurt, embrace each other as if they were entering into each other's bodies either while the woman is sitting on the lap of the man or in front of him, or on a bed,

then it is called an embrace like a
"mixture of milk and water."

These two embraces take place at the
time of the sexual union.

Babhravya has thus related to us the
above eight kinds of embraces.

Suvarnanabha, moreover, gives us four
ways of embracing simple members
of the body, which are:

> The embrace of the thighs
>
> The embrace of the *jaghana*,
> that is, the part of the body from
> the navel downward
> to the thighs
>
> The embrace of the breasts
>
> The embrace of the forehead

On the Embrace

When a man and a woman are very much in love . . . embrace each other as if they were entering into each other's bodies either while the woman is sitting on the lap of the man or in front of him, or on a bed, then it is called an embrace like a "mixture of milk and water."

1   When one of two lovers presses
    forcibly one or both of the thighs of
    the other between his or her own, it is
    called the "embrace of the thighs."

2   When the man presses the jaghana, or
    middle part, of the woman's body
    against his own, and mounts upon
    her to practice, either scratching with
    the nail or finger, or biting or striking
    or kissing, the hair of the woman
    being loose and flowing, it is called the
    "embrace of the jaghana."

3   When a man places his breast
    between the breasts of a woman and
    presses her with it, it is called the
    "embrace of the breasts."

4   When either of the lovers touches the
    mouth, the eyes, and the forehead of
    the other with his or her own, it is
    called the "embrace of the forehead."

On the Embrace

Some say that even shampooing is a kind of embrace, because there is a touching of bodies in it. But Vatsyayana thinks that shampooing is performed at a different time, and for a different purpose; and as it is also of a different character, it cannot be said to be included in the embrace. There are also some verses on the subject, as follows:

> "Embracing is of such a nature that men who ask questions about it acquire thereby a desire for enjoyment."

"The whole subject of embracing is of such nature that men who ask questions about it, or who hear about it, or who talk about it, acquire thereby a desire for enjoyment. Even those embraces that are not mentioned in the *Kama Shastra* should be practiced at the time of sexual enjoyment, if they are in any way conducive to the increase of love or passion. The rules of the Shastra apply as long as the passion of man is middling, but when the wheel of love is once set in motion, there is then no Shastra and no order."

On the Embrace

On Kissing

I t is said by some that there is no fixed time or order between the embrace, the kiss, and the pressing or scratching with the nails or fingers, but that all these things should be done generally before sexual union takes place, while striking and making the various sounds generally takes place at the time of the union. Vatsyayana, however, thinks that anything may take place at any time, for love does not care for time or order.

On the occasion of first congress, kissing and the other things mentioned above should be done moderately, they should not be continued for a long time, and should be done alternately. On subsequent occasions, however, the reverse of all this may take place, and moderation will not be necessary; they may continue for a long time; and for the purpose of kindling love, they may be all done at the same time.

The following are the places for kissing: the forehead, the eyes, the cheeks, the throat, the bosom, the breasts, the lips, and the interior of the mouth. Moreover, the people of the Lat country kiss also the following places: the joints of the thighs, the arms, and the navel. But Vatsyayana thinks that though kissing is practiced by these people in the above places because of the intensity of their love and the customs of their country, it is not fit to be practiced by all.

Now, with a young girl there are three sorts of kisses:

The nominal kiss

The throbbing kiss

The touching kiss

When a girl touches only the mouth of her lover with her own, but does not herself do anything, it is called the "nominal kiss."

When a girl, setting aside her bashfulness a little, wishes to touch the lip that is pressed into her mouth, and with that object moves her lower lip, but not the upper one, it is called the "throbbing kiss."

> When the lips of two lovers are brought into contact... it is called a "straight kiss."

anskrit Translation:
.nything goes. Because
assion waits for no one.
o says Vatsyayana.

When a girl touches her lover's lip
with her tongue, and having shut her
eyes, places her hands on those of her
lover, it is called the "touching kiss."

Other authors describe four other
kinds of kisses:

> The straight kiss
>
> The bent kiss
>
> The turned kiss
>
> The pressed kiss

1   When the lips of two lovers are
    brought into direct contact with each
    other, it is called a "straight kiss."

2   When the heads of two lovers are
    bent toward each other, and when
    so bent, kissing takes place, it is
    called a "bent kiss."

On Kissing

3   When one of them turns up the face
    of the other by holding the head and
    chin, and then kissing it, it is called a
    "turned kiss."

4   Lastly, when the lower lip is pressed
    with much force, it is called the
    "pressed kiss."

    There is also a fifth kind of kiss,
    called the "greatly pressed kiss,"
    which is effected by taking hold of
    the lower lip between two fingers, and
    then after touching it with the
    tongue, pressing it with great force
    with the lip.

    As regards kissing, a wager may be
    laid as to which will get hold of the
    lips of the other first. If the woman
    loses, she should pretend to cry,
    should keep her lover off by shaking
    her hands, and turn away from him

and dispute with him, saying, "Let another wager be laid." If she loses this a second time, she should appear doubly distressed, and when her lover is off his guard or asleep, she should get hold of his lower lip, and hold it in her teeth, so that it should not slip away; and then she should laugh, make a loud noise, deride him, dance about, and say whatever she likes in a joking way, moving her eyebrows, and rolling her eyes. Such are the wagers and quarrels as far as kissing is concerned, but the same may be applied with regard to the pressing or scratching with the nails and fingers, biting and striking. All these, however, are peculiar only to men and women of intense passion.

> As regards kissing a wager may be laid as to which will get hold of the lips of the other first.

When a man kisses the upper lip of a woman, while she in return kisses his lower lip, it is called the "kiss of the upper lip."

When one of them takes both the lips of the other between his or her own, it is called a "clasping kiss." A woman, however, takes this kind of a kiss only from a man who has no moustache. And on the occasion of this kiss, if one of them touches the teeth, the tongue, and the palate of the other, with his or her tongue, it is called the "fighting of the tongue." In the same way, the pressing of the teeth of the one against the mouth of the other is to be practiced.

Kissing is of four kinds: moderate, contracted, pressed, and soft, according to the different parts of the body which are kissed, for different kinds of kisses are appropriate for different parts of the body.

When a woman looks at the face of her lover while he is asleep, and kisses it to show her intention or desire, it is called a "kiss that kindles love."

When a woman kisses her lover while he is engaged in business, or while he is quarreling with her, or while he is looking at something else, so that his mind may be turned away, it is called a "kiss that turns away."

When a lover coming home late at night kisses his beloved who is asleep on her bed, in order to show her his desire, it is called a "kiss that awakens." On such an occasion the woman may pretend to be asleep at the time of her lover's arrival, so that she may

When a lover
coming home late
at night kisses his
beloved who is asleep
on her bed, in order
to show her his
desire, it is called a
"kiss that awakens."

104

know his intention and obtain respect from him.

When a person kisses the reflection of the person he loves in a mirror, in water, or on a wall, it is called a "kiss showing the intention."

"Whatever things may be done by one of the lovers to the other, the same should be returned."

When a person kisses a child sitting on his lap, or a picture or an image or figure, in the presence of the person beloved by him, it is called a "transferred kiss."

When at night at a theater, or in an assembly of caste men, a man coming up to a woman kisses a finger of her hand if she be standing, or a toe of her foot if she be sitting, or when a woman in shampooing her lover's body places her face in his thigh (as if she were sleepy) so as to inflame his passion, and kisses his thigh or great toe, it is called a "demonstrative kiss."

There is also a verse on this subject as follows:

"Whatever things may be done by one of the lovers to the other, the same should be returned by the other; that is, if the woman kisses him he should kiss her in return; if she strikes him he should also strike her in return."

On Kissing

On Pressing or Marking or Scratching With the Nails

hen love becomes intense, pressing with the nails or scratching the body with them is practiced, and it is done on the following occasions: on the first visit; at the time of setting out on a journey; on the return from a journey; at the time when an angry lover is reconciled; and, lastly, when the woman is intoxicated.

But pressing with the nails is not a usual thing except with those who are intensely passionate. It is employed, together with biting, by those to whom the practice is agreeable.

On Pressing or Marking or Scratching With the Nails

Pressing with the nails is of the eight
following kinds, according to the forms
of the marks which are produced:

1 Sounding

2 Half-moon

3 A circle

4 A line

5 A tiger's nail or claw

6 A peacock's foot

7 The jump of a hare

8 The leaf of a blue lotus

The places that are to be pressed with
the nails are: the armpit, the throat,
the breasts, the lips, the jaghana, or
middle parts of the body, and the
thighs. But Suvarnanabha is of the

opinion that when the impetuosity of passion is excessive, then the places need not be considered.

The qualities of good nails are that they should be bright, well set, clean, entire, convex, soft, and glossy in appearance. Nails are of three kinds according to their size:

Small

Middling

Large

Large nails, which give grace to the hands, and attract the hearts of women from their appearance, are possessed by the Bengalese.

Small nails, which can be used in various ways, and are to be applied only with the object of giving pleasure, are possessed by the people of the southern districts.

Middling nails, which contain the properties of both the above kinds, belong to the people of Maharashtra.

1 When a person presses the chin, the breasts, the lower lip, or the jaghana of another so softly that no scratch or mark is left, but only the hair on the body becomes erect from the touch of the nails, and the nails themselves make a sound, it is called a "sounding or pressing with the nails."

This pressing is used in the case of a young girl when her lover shampoos her, scratches her head, and wants to trouble or frighten her.

2 The curved mark with the nails, which is impressed on the neck and the breasts, is called the "half-moon."

On Pressing or Marking or Scratching With the Nails

3   When the half-moons are impressed
    opposite each other, it is called "a cir-
    cle." This mark with the nails is gen-
    erally made on the navel, the small
    cavities about the buttocks, and on
    the joints of the thigh.

4   A mark in the form of a small line,
    which can be made on any part of
    the body, is called a "line."

5   This same line, when it is curved,
    and made on the breast, is called a
    "tiger's nail."

6   When a curved mark is made on the
    breast by means of the five nails, it
    is called a "peacock's foot." This mark
    is made with the object of being
    praised, for it requires a great deal
    of skill to make it properly.

7   When five marks with the nails are

made close to one another near the nipple of the breast, it is called "the jump of a hare."

8 A mark made on the breast or on the hips in the form of a leaf of the blue lotus is called the "leaf of a blue lotus."

When a person is going on a journey, and makes a mark on the thighs, or on the breast, it is often called a "token of remembrance." On such an occasion three or four lines are impressed close to one another with the nails.

Here ends discourse of the marking with the nails. Marks of kinds other than the above may also be made with the nails, for the ancient authors say that there are innumerable degrees of skill among men (the practice of this art being known to all), so there are innumerable ways of making these

A mark made
on the breast or on
the hips in the form
of a leaf of the blue
lotus is called the
"leaf of a blue lotus."

marks. And as pressing or marking with the nails is dependent on love, no one can say with certainty how may different kinds of marks with the nails do actually exist. The reason for this is, Vatsyayana says, that as a variety is necessary in love, so love is to be produced by means of variety. It is on this account that courtesans, who are well acquainted with various ways and means, become so desirable; for if variety is sought in all the arts and amusements, such as archery and others, how much more should it be sought after in the art of love.

The marks of the nails should not be made on married women, but particular kinds of marks may be made on their private parts for the remembrance and increase of love.

There are also some verses on the subject, as follows:

"The love of a woman who sees the marks of nails on the private parts of her body, even though they are old and almost worn out, becomes again fresh and new. If there be no marks of nails to remind a person of the passages of love, the love is lessened in the same way as when no union takes place for a long time."

Even when a stranger sees at a distance a young woman with the marks of nails on her breast,[1] he is filled with love and respect for her.

A man, also, who carries the marks of nails and teeth on some parts of his body, influences the mind of a woman, even though it be ever so firm. In short, nothing tends to increase love so much as the effects of marking with the nails, and biting.

1 From this it would appear that in ancient times the breasts of women were not covered, and this is seen in the painting of the Ajanta and other caves, where we find that the breasts of even royal ladies and others are exposed.

"The love of a
woman who sees
the marks of nails
on the private parts
of her body...
becomes again
fresh and
new."

On Biting, and the Means to Be Employed With Regard to Women of Different Countries

ll the places that can be kissed are also the places that can be bitten, except the upper lip, the interior of the mouth, and the eyes.

The qualities of good teeth are as follows: They should be equal, possessed of a pleasing brightness, capable of being colored, of proper proportions, unbroken, and with sharp ends.

The defects of teeth, on the other hand, are that they are blunt, protruding from the gums, rough, soft, large, and loosely set.

On Biting, and the Means to Be Employed With
Regard to Women of Different Countries

The following are the different kinds of biting:

The hidden bite

The swollen bite

The point

The line of points

The coral and the jewel

The line of jewels

The broken cloud

The biting of the boat

All places that can be kissed are also the places that can be bitten, except the upper lip, the interior of the mouth, and the eyes.

1 The biting which is shown only by the excessive redness of the skin that is bitten, is called the "hidden bite."

2 When the skin is pressed down on both sides, it is called the "swollen bite."

کوی از بس نشاط کنیز پرواز کبوتر چهره شد بر سینه باز
کوزن ماده میکوشید باشه

مرو هم شیر نرشد عاقبت
با قوت ارعقیقش مهربرد

شکرخی کرد و تا خازن نهشت

3 When a small portion of the skin is bitten with two teeth only, it is called "the point."

4 When such small portions of the skin are bitten with all the teeth, it is called the "line of points."

5 The biting which is done by bringing together the teeth and the lips is called the "coral and the jewel." The lips are the coral, and the teeth are the jewel.

6 When biting is done with all the teeth, it is called the "line of jewels."

7 The biting which consists of unequal risings in a circle and which comes from the space between the teeth, is called the "broken cloud." This is impressed on the breasts.

8   The biting which consists of many broad rows of marks near to one another, and with red intervals, is called the "biting of a boar." This is impressed on the breasts and the shoulders; and these two last modes of biting are peculiar to persons of intense passion.

The lower lip is the place on which the "hidden bite," the "swollen bite," and the "point" are made; the "swollen bite" and the "coral and the jewel" bite are done on the cheek. Kissing, pressing with the nails, and biting are the ornaments of the left cheek, and when the word "cheek" is used, it is understood as the left cheek.

> When small portions of the skin are bitten with all the teeth, it is called the "line of points."

Both the "line of points" and the "line

On Biting, and the Means to Be Employed With Regard to Women of Different Countries

of jewels" are to be impressed on the throat, the armpit, and the joints of the thighs; but the "line of points" alone is to be impressed on the forehead and the thighs.

The marking with the nails, and the biting of the following things, namely an ornament of the forehead, an ear ornament, a bunch of flowers, a betel leaf, or a tamala leaf, which are worn by or belong to the woman who is beloved, are signs of desire of enjoyment.

Here ends discourse of the different kinds of biting.

In the affairs of love a man should do such things as are agreeable to the women of different countries.

The women of central countries (that is, between the Ganges and the

Jumna) are noble in their character, not accustomed to disgraceful practices, and dislike pressing with the nails and biting.

The women of the Balhika country are gained over by striking.

The women of Avantika are fond of foul pleasures, and have not good manners.

The women of Maharashtra are fond of practicing the sixty-four arts; they utter low and harsh words, and like to be spoken to in the same way, and have an impetuous desire of enjoyment.

The women of Pataliputra (that is, the modern Patna) are of the same nature as the women of the Maharashtra, but show their likings only in secret.

The women of the Dravidian country, though they are rubbed and pressed about at the time of sexual enjoyment, have a slow fall of semen; that is, they are very slow in the act of coition.

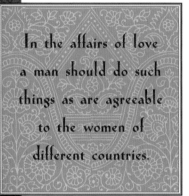

In the affairs of love a man should do such things as are agreeable to the women of different countries.

The women of Vanavasi are moderately passionate; they go through every kind of enjoyment, cover their bodies, and abuse those who utter low, mean, and harsh words.

The women of Avanti hate kissing, marking with the nails, and biting, but they have a fondness for various kinds of sexual union.

The women of Malwa like embracing and kissing, but not wounding, and they are gained over by striking.

The women of Abhira, and those of the country about the Indus and five rivers (that is, the Punjab), are gained over by the Auparishtaka, or mouth congress.

The women of Aparatika are full of passion, and make slowly the sound *Sit*.

The women of the Lat country have even more impetuous desire, and also make the sound *Sit*.

The women of the Stri Rajya and of Koshala (Oudh) are full of impetuous desire; their semen falls in large quantities, and they are fond of taking medicine to make it do so.

The women of the Andhra country

On Biting, and the Means to Be Employed With Regard to Women of Different Countries

have tender bodies; they are fond of enjoyment, and have a liking for voluptuous pleasures.

The women of Gandak have tender bodies, and speak sweetly.

Now, Suvarnanabha is of opinion that that which is agreeable to the nature of a particular person is of more consequence than that which is agreeable to a whole nation, and that therefore the peculiarities of the country should not be observed in such cases. The various pleasures, the dress, and the sports of one country are in time borrowed by another, and in such a case these things must be considered as belonging originally to that country.

Among the things mentioned above, namely, embracing, kissing, and so on, those which increase passion

AMONG the thiNGs MENtioNEd abovE, NAMElY, EMbRaciNG, kissiNG, aNd so oN, those which iNcREasE passioN should bE doNE first.

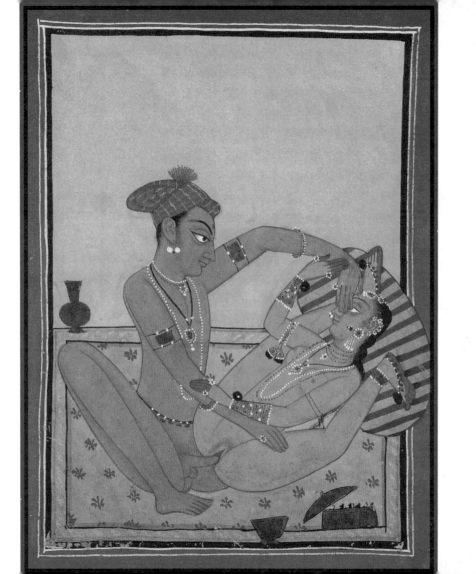

should be done first, and those which are only for amusement or variety should be done afterward.

There are also some verses on this subject, as follows:

"When a man bites a woman forcibly, she should angrily do the same to him with double force. Thus a 'point' should be returned with a 'line of points,' and a 'line of points' with a 'broken cloud'; and if she be excessively chaffed, she should at once begin a quarrel with him. At such a time she should take hold of her lover by the hair, and bend his head down, and kiss his lower lip, and then, being intoxicated with love, she should shut her eyes and bite him in various places. Even by day and in a place of public resort, when her lover shows her any mark that she may have inflicted on his body, she should smile at the sight of it, and turning her face as if she were going to chide him, she should show him with an angry look the marks on her own body that have been made by him. Thus if men and women act according to each other's liking, their love for each other will not be lessened even in one hundred years."

On Biting, and the Means to Be Employed With Regard to Women of Different Countries

On the Various Ways of Lying Down, and the Different Kinds of Congress

n the occasion of a "high congress" the Mrigi (Deer) woman should lie down in such a way as to widen her yoni, while in a "low congress" the Hastini (Elephant) woman should lie down so as to contract hers. But in an "equal congress" they should lie down in the natural position. What is said above concerning the Mrigi and the Hastini applies also to the Vadawa (Mare) woman. In a "low congress" the woman should particularly make use of medicine, to cause her desires to be satisfied quickly.

The Deer woman has the following

On the Various Ways of Lying Down,
and the Differnt Kinds of Congress

three ways of lying down:

The widely opened position

The yawning position

The position of the wife of Indra

When she lowers her head and raises her middle parts, it is called the "widely opened position." At such a time the man should apply some unguent, so as to make the entrance easy.

When she raises her thighs and keeps them wide apart and engages in congress, it is called the "yawning position."

When she places her thighs with her legs doubled on them upon her sides, and thus engages in congress, it is called the position of Indrani, and this is learned only by practice. The position is also useful in the case of the "highest congress."

When she raises her thighs and keeps them wide apart and engages in congress, it is called the "yawning position."

There are also the "clasping position" and the "low congress," and in the "lowest congress," together with the "pressing position," the "twining position," and the "mare's position."

When the legs of both the male and the female are stretched straight out over each other, it is called the "clasping position." It is of two kinds, the side position and the supine position, according to the way in which they lie down. In the side position the male should invariably lie on his left side, and cause the woman to lie on her right side, and this rule is to be observed in lying down with all kinds of women.

When, after congress has begun in the clasping position, the woman presses her lover with her thighs, it is called the "pressing position."

When the woman places one of her thighs across the thigh of her lover, it is called the "twining position."

When the woman forcibly holds in her yoni the lingam after it is in, it is called the "mare's position." This is learned by practice only, and is chiefly found among the women of the Andra country.

The above are the different ways of lying down, mentioned by Babhravya; Suvarnanabha, however, gives the following in addition:

When the female raises both of her thighs straight up, it is called the "rising position."

When she raises both of her legs, and places them on her lover's shoulders, it is called the "yawning position."

When the legs are contracted, and thus held by the lover before his bosom, it is called the "pressed position."

When only one of her legs is stretched out, it is called the "half-pressed position."

When the woman places one of her legs on her lover's shoulder, and stretches the other out, and then places the latter on his shoulder, and stretches out the other, and continues to do so alternately, it is called the "splitting of a bamboo."

When one of her legs is placed on the head, and the other is stretched out, it is called the "fixing of a nail." This is learned by practice only.

When both the legs of the woman are contracted, and placed on her stomach,

When both the legs of the woman are contracted, and placed on her stomach, it is called the "crab's position."

it is called the "crab's position."

When the thighs are raised and placed one upon the other, it is called the "packed position."

When the shanks are placed one upon the other, it is called the "lotus-like position."

When a man, during congress, turns round, and enjoys the woman without leaving her, while she embraces him round the back all the time, it is called the "turning position," and is learned only by practice.

Thus, says Suvarnanabha, these different ways of lying down, sitting, and standing should be practiced in water, because it is easy to do so therein. But Vatsyayana is of opinion that congress in water is improper because it is prohibited by religious law.

When a man and a woman support themselves on each other's bodies, or on a wall or pillar, and thus while standing engage in congress, it is called the "supported congress."

When a man supports himself against a wall, and the woman, sitting on his hands joined together and held underneath her, throws her arms round his neck and putting her thighs alongside his waist, moves herself by her feet, which are touching the wall against which the man is leaning, it is called the "suspended congress."

When a woman stands on her hands and feet like a quadruped, and her lover mounts her like a bull, it is called the "congress of a cow." At this time everything that is ordinarily done on the bosom should be done on the back.

In the same way can be carried on the congress of a dog, the congress of a goat, the congress of a deer, the forcible mounting of an ass, the congress of a cat, the jump of a tiger, the pressing of an elephant, the rubbing of a boar, and the mounting of a horse. And in all these cases the characteristics of the different animals should be manifested by acting like them.

"An ingenious person should multiply the kinds of congress after the fashion of the different kinds of beasts and birds."

When a man enjoys two women at the same time, both of whom love him equally, it is called the "united congress."

When a man enjoys many women altogether, it is called the "congress of a herd of cows."

The following kinds of congress, namely, sporting in water, or the congress of an elephant with many female elephants which is said to take place only in the water, the congress of a collection of goats, the congress of a collection of deer, take place in imitation of these animals.

In Gramaneri many young men enjoy a woman that may be married to one of them, either one after the other or at the same time. Thus one of them holds her, another enjoys her, a third uses her mouth, a fourth holds her middle part, and in this way they go on enjoying her several parts alternately.

The same things can be done when

When a man enjoys
two women at the
same time it is called
the "united congress."

several men are sitting in company with one courtesan, or when one courtesan is alone with many men. In the same way this can be done by the women of the king's harem when they accidentally get hold of a man.

The people in the Southern countries have also a congress in the anus, that is called the "lower congress."

Thus ends the various kinds of congress. There are also two verses on the subjects, as follows:

"An ingenious person should multiply the kinds of congress after the fashion of the different kinds of beasts and of birds. For these different kinds of congress, performed according to the usage of each country, and the liking of each individual, generate love, friendship, and respect in the hearts of women."

On the Various Modes of Striking, and on the Sounds Appropriate to Them

Sexual intercourse can be compared to a quarrel, on account of the contrarieties of love and its tendency to dispute. The place of striking with passion is the body, and on the body the special places are:

The shoulders
The head
The space between the breasts
The back
The jaghana, or middle part of the body
The sides

Striking is of four kinds:

Striking with the back of the hand
Striking with the fingers a little contracted

*On the Various Modes of Striking,
and on the Sounds Appropriate to Them*

Striking with the fist

Striking with the open palm of the hand

On account of its causing pain, striking gives rise to the kissing sound,
which is of various kinds, and to the
eight kinds of crying:

The sound *Hin*

The thundering sound

The cooing sound

The weeping sound

The sound *Phut*

The sound *Phāt*

The sound *Sūt*

The sound *Plāt*

Besides these, there are also words
having a meaning, such as "mother,"
and those that are expressive of prohibition, sufficiency, desire of liberation,

pain or praise, and to
which may be added
sounds like those of the
dove, the cuckoo, the
green pigeon, the parrot,
the bee, the sparrow, the
flamingo, the duck, and
the quail, which are all
occasionally made use of.

The space between
the breasts should be
struck with the back
of the hand.

Blows with the fist
should be given on the
back of the woman, while she is sitting
on the lap of the man, and she should
give blows in return, abusing the man
as if she were angry, and making the
cooing and weeping sounds. While the
woman is engaged in congress the
space between the breasts should be
struck with the back of the hand, slowly at first, and then proportionately to
the increasing excitement, until the end.

*On the Various Modes of Striking,
and on the Sounds Appropriate to Them*

At this time the sounds *Hin* and others may be made, alternately or optionally, according to habit. When the man, making the sound *Phāt*, strikes the woman on the head with the fingers of his hand a little contracted, it is called Prasritaka, which means striking with the fingers of the hand a little contracted. In this case the appropriate sounds are the cooing sound, the sound *Phāt*, and the sound *Phut* in the interior of the mouth, and at the end of congress the sighing and weeping sounds. The sound *Phāt* is an imitation of the sound of a bamboo being split, while the sound *Phut* is like the sound of something falling into water. At all times when kissing

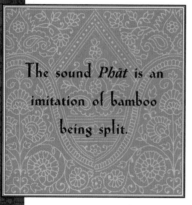

The sound *Phāt* is an imitation of bamboo being split.

and suchlike things are begun, the woman should give a reply with a kissing sound. During the excitement, when a woman is not accustomed to striking, she continually utters words expressive of prohibition, sufficiency, or desire of liberation, as well as the words "father," "mother," intermingled with the sighing, weeping, and thundering sound. Toward the conclusion of the congress, the breasts, the jaghana, and the sides of the women should be pressed with the open palms of the hand, with some force, until the end of it, and then sounds like those of the quail or the goose should be made.

There are also two verses on the subject, as follows:

"The characteristics of manhood are said to consist of roughness and impetuosity, while weakness, tenderness, sensibility, and an inclination to turn away from unpleasant things are the distinguishing marks of womanhood. The excitement of passion, and peculiarities of habit, may sometimes cause contrary results to appear, but these do not last long, and in the end the natural state is resumed."

The wedge on the bosom, the scissors on the head, the piercing instrument on the cheeks, and the pincers on the breasts and sides may also be taken into consideration with the other four modes of striking, and thus give eight ways altogether. But these four ways of striking with instruments are peculiar to the people of the southern countries, and the marks caused by them are seen on the breasts of their women. They are local peculiarities, but Vatsyayana is of the opinion that the practice of them is painful, barbarous, and base, and quite unworthy of imitation.

In the same way anything that is a local peculiarity should not always be adopted elsewhere, and even in the place when the practice is prevalent, excess of it should always be avoided. Instances of the dangerous use of them may be given as follows. The King of the Panchalas killed the courtesan Madhavasena by means of the wedge during congress. King Satakarni Satavahana of the Kuntala, deprived his great Queen Malayavati of her life by a pair of scissors, and Naradeva, whose hand was deformed, blinded a dancing girl by directing a piercing instrument in a wrong way.

There are also two verses on the subject, as follows:

"About these things there cannot be either enumeration or any definite rule. Congress having once commenced, passion alone gives birth to all the acts of the parties."

Such passionate actions and amorous gesticulations or movements, which arise on the spur of the moment, and during sexual intercourse, cannot be defined, and are as irregular as dreams. A horse having once attained the fifth degree of motion goes on with blind speed, regardless of pits, ditches, and posts in his way; and in the same manner a loving pair become blind with passion in the heat of congress, and go on with great impetuosity, paying not the least

"Congress having once commenced, passion alone gives birth to all the acts of the parties."

On the Various Modes of Striking, and on the Sounds Appropriate to Them

Such passionate
actions and amorous
gesticulations or
movements, which
arise on the spur of
the moment, and
during sexual inter-
course, cannot be
defined, and are as
irregular as dreams.

regard to excess. For this reason one who is well acquainted with the science of love, and knowing his own strength as also the tenderness, impetuosity, and strength of the young woman, should act accordingly. The various modes of enjoyment are not for all times or for all persons, but should be used only at the proper time, and in the proper countries and places.

On the Various Modes of Striking,
and on the Sounds Appropriate to Them

ON WOMEN ACTING THE PART
OF A MAN, AND ON THE WORK
OF A MAN

hen a woman sees that her lover is
fatigued by constant congress, without having his desire satisfied, she
should, with his permission, lay him
down upon his back, and give him
assistance by acting his part. She may
also do this to satisfy the curiosity of
her lover, or her own desire of novelty.

There are two ways of doing this: the
first is when during congress she
turns round, and gets on top of her
lover, in such a manner as to continue
the congress, without obstructing the
pleasure of it; and the other is when

On Women Acting the Part of a Man;
and on the Work of a Man

she acts the man's part from the beginning. At such a time, with flowers in her hair hanging loose, and her smiles broken by hard breathings, she should press her lover's bosom with her own breasts; and, lowering her head frequently, she should do in return the same actions which he used to do before, returning his blows and chaffing him. She should say, "I was laid down by you, and fatigued with hard congress; I shall now therefore lay you down in return." She should then again manifest her own bashfulness, her fatigue, and her desire of stopping the congress. In this way she should do the work of a man, which we shall presently relate.

Whatever is done by a man for giving pleasure to a woman is called the work of a man, and is as follows:

While the woman is lying on his bed, and is as it were abstracted by his conversation, he should loosen the knot of her undergarments, and when she begins to dispute with him he should overwhelm her with kisses. Then when his lingam is erect he should touch her with his hands in various places, and gently manipulate various parts of the body. If the woman is bashful, and if it is the first time that they have come together, the man should place his hands between her thighs, which she would probably keep close together; and if she is a very young girl, he should first get his hands upon her breasts, which she would probably cover with her own hands, and under her armpits and on her neck. If, however, she is a seasoned woman, he should do whatever is agreeable either to him or to her, and whatever is fitting for the occasion. After this, he should take hold of her hair, and hold her chin in his fingers for the purpose of kissing her. On this, if she is a young girl, she will become bashful and close her eyes. In any event, he should gather from the action of the woman what things would be pleasing to her during congress.

Here Suvarnanabha says that while a man is doing to the woman what he likes best during congress, he should always make a point of pressing those parts of her body on which she turns her eyes.

The signs of the enjoyment and satisfaction of the woman are as follows: her body relaxes, she closes her eyes, she puts aside all bashfulness, and shows increased willingness to unite the two organs as closely together as possible. On the other hand, the signs of her want of enjoyment and of failing to be satisfied are as follows: she shakes her hands, she does not let the man get up, feels dejected, bites the man, kicks him, and continues to go on moving after the man has finished. In such cases the man should rub the yoni of the woman with his hand and fingers (as the elephant rubs anything with his trunk) before engaging in congress, until it is softened, and after that is done he should proceed to put his lingam into her.

The acts to be done by the man are:

Moving forward

Friction or churning

Piercing

Rubbing

Pressing

Giving a blow
The blow of a boar
The blow of a bull
The sporting of a sparrow

1 When the organs are brought together properly and directly, it is called
   "moving the organ forward."

2 When the lingam is held with the
   hand, and turned all around in the
   yoni, it is called a "churning."

3 When the yoni is lowered, and the
   upper part is struck with the lingam,
   it is called "piercing."

4 When the same thing is done on the
   lower part of the yoni, it is called
   "rubbing."

On Women Acting the Part of a Man;
and on the Work of a Man

5   When the yoni is pressed by the lingam for a long time, it is called "pressing."

6   When the lingam is removed to some distance from the yoni, and then forcibly strikes it, it is called "giving a blow."

7   When only one part of the yoni is rubbed with the lingam, it is called "the blow of a boar."

8   When both sides of the yoni are rubbed in this way, it is called the "blow of a bull."

9   When the lingam is in the yoni, and is moved up and down frequently, and without being taken out, it is called the "sporting of a sparrow." This takes place at the end of congress.

When a woman acts the part of a man, she has the following things to do in addition to the nine given above:

The pair of tongs

The top

The swing

1 When the woman holds the lingam in her yoni, draws it in, presses it, and keeps it thus in her for a long time, it is called the "pair of tongs."

2 When, while engaged in congress, she turns round like a wheel, it is called the "top." This is learned by practice only.

3 When, on such an occasion, the man lifts up the middle part of his body, and the woman turns round her middle part, it is called the "swing."

On Women Acting the Part of a Man; and on the Work of a Man

When the woman is tired, she should place her forehead on that of her lover, and should thus take rest without disturbing the union of the organs; and when the woman has rested herself the man should turn round and begin the congress again.

There are also some verses on the subject, as follows:

"Though a woman is reserved, and keeps her feelings concealed, yet when she gets on top of a man, she then shows all her love and desire. A man should gather from the actions of the woman of what disposition she is, and in what way she likes to be enjoyed. A woman during her monthly courses, a woman who has been lately confined, and a fat woman should not be made to act the part of a man."

On the Auparishtaka,[1] or Mouth Congress

he Acharyas (ancient and venerable authors) are of opinion that this Auparishtaka is the work of a dog and of a man, because it is a low practice, and opposed to the orders of the Holy Writ (Dharma Shastras), and because the man himself suffers by bringing his lingam into contact with the mouths of eunuchs and women. But Vatsyayana says that the orders of the Holy Writ do not affect those who resort to courtesans, and the law prohibits the practice of the Auparishtaka with married women

This practice appears to have been prevalent in some parts of India from a very ancient time. The

On the Auparishtaka, or Mouth Congress

only. As regards the injury to the male, that can be easily remedied.

The people of eastern India do not resort to women who practice the Auparishtaka.

The people of Ahichhatra resort to such women, but do nothing with them so far as the mouth is concerned.

The people of Saketa do with these women every kind of mouth congress, while the people of Nagara do not practice this, but do every other thing.

The people of the Shurasena country, on the southern bank of Jumna, do everything without any hesitation, for they say that women being naturally unclean, no one can be certain about their character, their purity, their con-

Shushruta', a work on medicine some two thousand years old, describes the wounding of the lingam with the teeth as one of the cause of a disease treated upon in that work. Traces of the practice are found as far back as the eighth century, for various kind of the Auparishtaka are represented in the sculptures of many Shaivite temples at Bhubaneshwar near Cuttack, in Orissa, which were built about that period. From these sculptures being found in such places, it would seem that this practice was popular in that part of the country at that time. It does not seem to be so prevalent now in Hindustan, its place perhaps being supplanted by the practice of sodomy introduced since the Muslim period.

duct, their practices, their confidences, or their speech. They are not, however, on this account to be abandoned, because religious law, on the authority of which they are reckoned pure, lays down that the udder of a cow is clean at the time of milking, though the mouth of a cow, and also the mouth of her calf, are considered unclean by the Hindus. Again, a dog is clean when he seizes a deer in hunting, though food touched by a dog is otherwise considered very unclean. A bird is clean when it causes a fruit to fall from a tree by pecking at it, though things eaten by crows and other birds are considered unclean. And the mouth of a woman is clean for kissing and suchlike

In all these things connected with love, everybody should act according to... his own inclination.

On the Auparishtaka, or Mouth Congress

things at the time of sexual intercourse. Vatsyayana, moreover, thinks that in all these things connected with love, everybody should act according to the custom of his country, and his own inclination.

There are also the following verses on the subject:

"The male servants of some men carry on the mouth congress with their masters. It is also practiced by some citizens, who know each other well, among themselves. Some women of the harem, when they are amorous, do the acts of the mouth on the yonis of one another, and some men do the same thing with women. The way of doing this (kissing the yoni) should be known from kissing the mouth. When a man and woman lie down in an inverted order, with

When a man and woman lie down in an inverted order, with the head of one toward the feet of the other, and carry on this congress, it is called the "congress of a crow."

the head of the one toward the feet of the other, and carry on this congress, it is called the "congress of a crow."

For the sake of such things, courtesans abandon men possessed of good qualities, liberal and clever, and become attached to low persons, such as slaves and elephant drivers. The Auparishtaka, or mouth congress, should never be done by a learned Brahmin, by a minister that carries on the business of a state, or by a man of good reputation, because though the practice is allowed by the Shastras, there is no reason why it should be carried on, and need be practiced only in particular cases. For instance, the taste and the digestive qualities of the flesh of dogs are mentioned in the works on medicine, but it does not therefore follow that it should be eaten by the wise. In the same way there are some men, some places, and some times with respect to which these practices can be made use of. A man should therefore pay regard to the place, to the time, and to the practice which is to be carried out, as also as to whether it is agreeable to his nature and to himself, and then he may or may not practice these things according to circumstances. But after all, these things being done secretly, and the mind of the man being fickle, how can it be known what any person will do at any particular time and for any particular purpose?"

On the Auparishtaka, or Mouth Congress

How to Begin and How to End the Congress, Different Kinds of Congress, and Love Quarrels

n the pleasure room, decorated with flowers, and fragrant with perfumes, attended by his friends and servants, the citizen should receive the woman, who will come bathed and dressed, and will invite her to take refreshment and to drink freely. He should then seat her on his left side, and holding her hair, and touching also the end and knot of her garment, he should gently embrace her with his right arm. They should then carry on amusing conversation on various subjects, and may also talk suggestively of

How to Begin and How to End the Congress;
Different Kinds of Congress, and Love Quarrels

things which would be considered as coarse, or not to be mentioned generally in society. They may then sing, either with or without gesticulations, and play on musical instruments, talk about the arts, and persuade each other to drink. At last, when the woman is overcome with love and desire, the citizen should dismiss the people that may be with him, giving them flowers, ointments, and betel leaves; and then when the two are left alone, they should proceed as has been already described in the previous chapters.

Such is the beginning of the sexual union. At the end of the congress, the lovers, with modesty, and not looking at each other, should go separately to the washing room. After this, sitting in their own places, they should eat some betel leaves, and the citizen

At last, when the woman is overcome with love and desire, the citizen should dismiss the people; when the two are left alone, they should proceed as has been already described.

183

should apply with his own hand to the body of the woman some pure sandalwood ointment, or ointment of some other kind. He should then embrace her with his left arm, and with agreeable words should cause her to drink from a cup held in his own hand, or he may give her water to drink. They can then eat sweetmeats, or anything else, according to their liking, and may drink fresh juice,[1] soup, gruel, extracts of meat, sherbet, the juice of mango fruits, the extract of the juice of the citron tree mixed with sugar, or anything that may be liked in different countries, and known to be sweet, soft, and pure. The lovers may also sit on the terrace of the palace or house,

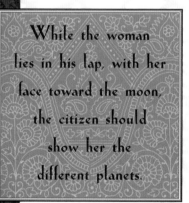

While the woman lies in his lap, with her face toward the moon, the citizen should show her the different planets.

and enjoy the moonlight, and carry on an agreeable conversation. At this time, too, while the woman lies in his lap, with her face toward the moon, the citizen should show her the different planets, the morning star, the polar star, and the seven Rishis, or Great Bear.

This is the end of sexual union.

Congress is of the following kinds:

Loving congress

Congress of subsequent love

Congress of artificial love

Congress of transferred love

Congress like that of eunuchs

Deceitful congress

Congress of spontaneous love

The fresh juice of the coconut tree, the date tree, and other kinds of palm trees are drunk in India. It will not keep very fresh very long, but ferments rapidly, and is then distilled into liquor.

How to Begin and How to End the Congress; Different Kinds of Congress, and Love Quarrels

1   When a man and a woman who have
    been in love with each other for some
    time come together with great diffi-
    culty, or when one of the two returns
    from a journey, or is reconciled after
    having been separated because of a
    quarrel, then congress is called the
    "loving congress." It is carried on
    according to the liking of the lovers,
    and for as long as they choose.

2   When two persons come together,
    while their love for each other is still
    in its infancy, their congress is called
    the "congress of subsequent love."

3   When a man carries on the congress
    by exciting himself by means of the
    sixty-four ways, such as kissing, and
    so on, or when a man and a woman
    come together, though in reality they
    are both attached to different persons,
    their congress is often called "congress

of artificial love." At this time all the ways and means mentioned in the *Kama Shastra* should be used.

4 When a man, from the beginning to the end of the congress, though having connection with the woman, thinks all the time he is enjoying another one whom he loves, it is called the "congress of transferred love."

5 Congress between a man and a female water carrier, or a female servant of a caste lower than his own, lasting only until the desire is satisfied, is called "congress like that of eunuchs." Here external touches, kisses, and manipulations are not to be employed.

6 The congress between a courtesan and a rustic, and that between citi-

How to Begin and How to End the Congress;
Different Kinds of Congress, and Love Quarrels

zens and the women of villages and bordering countries, are called "deceitful congress."

7 The congress that takes place between two persons who are attached to one another, and which is done according to their own liking, is called "spontaneous congress."

Thus ends discourse of the kinds of congress.

We shall now speak of love quarrels.

A woman who is very much in love with a man cannot bear to hear the name of her rival mentioned, or to have any conversation regarding her, or to be addressed by her name through mistake. If such takes place, a great quarrel arises, and the woman cries, becomes angry, tosses her hair about, strikes her lover, falls from her bed or seat, and, casting aside her garlands and ornaments, throws herself down on the ground.

At this time the lover should attempt to reconcile her with conciliatory words, and should take her up carefully and place her on her bed. But she, not replying to his questions, and with increased anger, should bend down his head by pulling his hair, and having kicked him once, twice, or thrice on his arms, head, bosom, or back, should then proceed to the door of the room. Dattaka says that she should then sit angrily near the door and shed tears, but should not go out,

> A woman who is very much in love with a man cannot bear to hear the name of her rival.

How to Begin and How to End the Congress;
Different Kinds of Congress, and Love Quarrels

because she would be found fault
with for going away. After a time,
when she thinks that the conciliatory
words and actions of her lover have
reached their utmost, she should then
embrace him, talking to him with
harsh and reproachful words, but at
the same time showing a loving desire
for congress.

When the woman is in her own
house, and has quarreled with her
lover, she should go to him and show
how angry she is, and leave him.
Afterward the citizen having sent the
Vita, the Vidushaka, or the
Pithamarda to pacify her, she should
accompany them back to the house,
and spend the night with her lover.

Thus ends the discourse of the love
quarrels.

How to Begin and How to End the Congress;
Different Kinds of Congress, and Love Quarrels

In conclusion:

A man employing the sixty-four means mentioned by Babhravya obtains his object, and enjoys the woman of the first quality. Though he may speak well on other subjects, if he does not know sixty-four divisions, no great respect is paid to him in the assembly of the learned. A man, devoid of other knowledge, but well acquainted with the sixty-four divisions, becomes a leader in any society of men and women. What man will not respect the sixty-four parts, considering they are respected by the learned, by the cunning, and by the courtesans? As the sixty-four parts

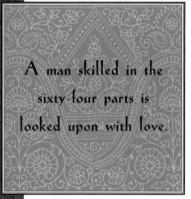

A man skilled in the sixty-four parts is looked upon with love.

are respected, are charming, and add to the talent of women, they are called by the Acharyas dear to women. A man skilled in the sixty-four parts is looked upon with love by his own wife, by the wives of others, and by courtesans.

ABOUT THE ACQUISITION
OF A WIFE

ON MARRIAGE

hen a girl of the same caste, and a virgin, is married in accordance with the precepts of Holy Writ (Dharma Shastras), the results of such a union are: the acquisition of Sharma and Artha, offspring, affinity, increase of friends, and untarnished love. For this reason a man should fix his affections upon a girl who is of good family, whose parents are alive, and who is three years or more younger than himself. She should be born of a highly respectable family, possessed of wealth, well connected, and with

On Marriage

many relations and friends. She should also be beautiful, of a good disposition, with lucky marks on her body, and with good hair, nails, teeth, ears, eyes, and breasts, neither more nor less than they ought to be, and no one of them entirely wanting, and not troubled with a sickly body. The man should, of course, also possess these qualities himself. But at all events, says Ghotakamukha, a girl who has been already joined with others (that is, no longer a maiden) should never be loved, for it would be reproachful to do such a thing.

Now, in order to bring about a marriage with a girl such as described above, the parents and relations of the man should exert themselves, as should such friends on both sides as may be desired to assist in the matter. These friends should bring to the

A girl should be taken as a wife, and given in marriage, when fortune, signs, omens, and the words of others are favorable.

notice of the girl's parents, the faults, both present and future, of all the other men that may wish to marry her, and should at the same time extol even to exaggeration all the excellences, ancestral and paternal, of their friend, so as to endear him to them, and particularly to those that may be liked by the girl's mother. One of the friends should also disguise himself as an astrologer, and declare the future good fortune and wealth of his friend by showing the existence of all the lucky omens[1] and signs,[2] the good influence of planets, the auspicious entrance of the sun into a sign of the Zodiac, propitious stars and fortunate marks on his body. Others again should rouse the jealousy of the girl's mother by telling her that their friend has a chance of getting from some other quarter an even better girl than hers.

Sanskrit Translation:

When choosing the bride —

The mother, father,

relatives, and any others

whose advice is taken

should make the enquiries.

A girl should be taken as a wife, and given in marriage, when fortune, signs, omens, and the words[3] of others are favorable, for, says Ghotakamukha, a man should not marry at any time he likes. A girl who is asleep, crying, or gone out of the house when sought in marriage, or who is betrothed to another, should not be married.

When a girl becomes marriageable her parents should dress her smartly, and should place her where she can be easily seen by all. Every afternoon, having dressed her and decorated her in a becoming manner, they should send here with her female companions to sports, sacrifices, and marriage ceremonies, and thus show her to advantage in society, because she is a kind of merchandise. They should also receive with kind words and signs of friendliness those of an auspicious

1 The flight of a bluejay on a person's left is considered a lucky omen when one starts on any business; the appearance of a cat before anyone at such a time is looked on as a bad omen. There are many omens of the same kind.

2 Such as the throbbing of the right eye of men and the left eye of women, etc.

3 Before anything is begun it is a custom to go early in the morning to a neighbor's house, and overhear the first words that may be spoken in his family, and according as the words heard are of good or bad import, so draw an inference as to the success or failure of the undertaking.

appearance who may come accompanied by their friends and relatives for the purpose of marrying the daughter; and, under some pretext or other having first dressed her becomingly, the parents should then present her to them. After this, they should await the pleasure of fortune, and with this object should appoint a future day on which a determination could be come to with regard to their daughter's marriage. On this occasion when the persons have come, the parents of the girl should ask them to bathe and dine, and should say, "Everything will take place at the proper time," and should not then comply with the request, but should settle the matter later.

> When a girl becomes marriageable her parents should... place her where she can be easily seen.

When a girl is thus acquired, either according to the custom of the country or according to his own desire, the man should marry her in accordance with the precepts of the Holy Writ, according to one of the four kinds of marriage.

Thus ends discourse of marriage.

There are also some verses on the subject, as follows:

"Amusement in society, such as completing verses begun by others, marriages, and auspicious ceremonies, should be carried on neither with superiors nor with inferiors, but with our equals. That should be known as a high connection when a man, after marrying a girl, has to serve her and her relatives afterward like a servant, and such a connection is censured by the good. On the other hand, that reproachable connection where a man, together with his relatives, lords it over his wife is called a low connection by the wise. But when both the man and the woman afford mutual pleasure to each other, and where the relatives on both sides pay respect to one another, such is called a connection in the proper sense of the word. Therefore a man should contract neither a high connection by which he is obliged to bow down afterward to his kinsmen, nor a low connection, which is universally reprehended by all."

WHEN both the MAN aNd the woMAN afford Mutual pleasure to each other, aNd where the relatives oN both sides pay respect to oNe aNother, such is called a coNNection iN the proper seNse of the word.

On Creating Confidence in the Girl

or the first three days after marriage, the girl and her husband should sleep on the floor, abstain from sexual pleasures, and eat their food without seasoning it either with alkali or salt. For the next seven days they should bathe amidst the sounds of auspicious musical instruments, should decorate themselves, dine together, and pay attention to their relatives as well as to those who may have come to witness their marriage.

This is applicable to persons of all castes. On the night of the tenth day

On Creating Confidence in the Girl

the man should begin in a lonely place with soft words, and thus create confidence in the girl. Some authors say that for the purpose of winning her over he should not speak to her for three days; but the followers of Babhravya are of the opinion that if the man does not speak with her for three days, the girl may be discouraged by seeing him spiritless, like a pillar, and becoming dejected, she may begin to despise him as a eunuch. Vatsyayana says that the man should begin to win her over, and to create confidence in her, but should abstain at first from sexual pleasures. Women being of a tender nature, want tender beginnings, and when they are forcibly approached by

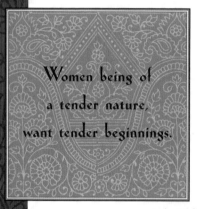

Women being of a tender nature, want tender beginnings.

men with whom they are but slightly acquainted, they sometimes suddenly become haters of sexual connection, and sometimes even haters of the male sex. The man should therefore approach the girl according to her liking, and should make use of those devices by which he may be able to establish himself more and more in her confidence. These devices are as follows:

He should embrace her first of all in the law she likes most, because it does not last for a long time.

He should embrace her with the upper part of his body, because that is easier and simpler. If the girl is grown up, or if the man has known her for some time, he may embrace her by the light of a lamp; but if he is not well acquainted with her, or if she is

On Creating Confidence in the Girl

a young girl, he should then embrace her in darkness.

When the girl accepts the embrace, the man should put a "tambula," or screw of betel nut and betel leaves, in her mouth, and if she will not take it, he should induce her to do so by conciliatory words, entreaties, oaths, and kneeling at her feet, for it is a universal rule that however bashful or angry a woman may be, she never disregards a man's kneeling at her feet. At the time of giving this tambula, he should kiss her mouth softly and gracefully, without making any sound. When she is gained over in this respect, he should then make her talk, and so that she may be induced to talk he should ask her questions about things of which he knows or pretends to know nothing, and which can be answered in a few words. If she does not speak to him, he should not frighten her, but should ask her the same thing again and again in a conciliatory manner. If she does not then speak, he should urge her to give a reply, because, as Ghotakamukha says, "All girls hear everything said to them by men, but do not themselves sometimes say a single word." When she is thus importuned, the girl should give replies by shakes of the head, but if she quarreled with the man she should not even do that. When she is asked by the man whether she desires him, and whether she likes him, she should remain silent for a long time, and when at last importuned to reply, should give him a favorable answer by a nod of her head. If the man is previously acquainted with the girl, he should converse with her by means of a female friend, who may

On Creating Confidence in the Girl

be favorable to him, and in the confidence of both, and carry on the conversation on both sides. On such an occasion the girl should smile with her head bent down, and if the female friend say more on her part than she was desired to do, she should chide her and dispute with her. The female friend should say in jest even what she is not desired to say by the girl, and add, "She says so"; on which the girl should say, indistinctly and prettily, "Oh, no! I did not say so," and she should then smile, and throw an occasional glance toward the man.

If the girl is familiar with the man, she should place near him, without saying anything, the tambula, the ointment, or the garland that he may have asked for, or she may tie them up in his upper garment. While she is engaged in this, the man should

The man should touch her young breasts in the sounding way of pressing with the nails, and if she prevents him doing this he should say to her, "I will not do it again if you will embrace me," and should in this way cause her to embrace him.

213

touch her young breasts in the sounding way of pressing with the nails, and if she prevents him doing this he should say to her, "I will not do it again if you will embrace me," and should in this way cause her to embrace him. While he is being embraced by her he should pass his hand repeatedly over and about her body. By and by he should place her in his lap, and try more and more to gain her consent, and if she will not yield to him he should frighten her by saying: "I shall impress marks of my teeth and nails upon your lips and breasts, and then make similar marks on my own body, and shall tell my friends that you did them. What will you say then?" In this and other ways, as fear and confidence are created in the minds of children, so should the man gain her over to his wishes.

On the second and third nights, after her confidence has increased still more, he should feel the whole of her body with his hands, and kiss her all over; he should also place his hands upon her thighs and shampoo them, and if he succeeds in this he should then shampoo the joints of her thighs. If she tries to prevent him doing this, he should say to her, "What harm is there in doing it?" and should persuade her to let him do it. After gaining this point he should touch her private parts, should loosen her girdle and the knot of her dress, and, turning up her lower garment, should shampoo the joints of her naked thighs. Under various pretenses he should do all these things,

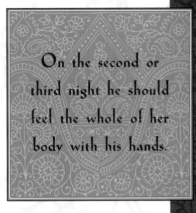

On the second or third night he should feel the whole of her body with his hands.

On Creating Confidence in the Girl

but he should not at that time begin actual congress. After this, he should teach her the sixty-four arts, should tell her how much he loves her, and describe to her the hopes he formerly entertained regarding her. He should also promise to be faithful to her in future, and should dispel all her fears with respect to rival women, and at last, after having overcome her bashfulness, he should begin to enjoy her in a way so as not to frighten her. So much about creating confidence in a girl; there are, moreover, some verses on the subject, as follows:

"A man acting according to the inclinations of a girl should try to gain her over so that she may love him and place her confidence in him. A man does not succeed either by implicitly following the inclination of a girl or by wholly opposing

her, and he should therefore adopt a middle course. He who knows how to make himself beloved by women, as well as to increase their honor and create confidence in them, becomes an object of their love. But he who neglects a girl, thinking she is too bashful, is despised by her as a beast ignorant of the working of the female mind. Moreover, a girl forcibly enjoyed by one who does not understand the hearts of girls become nervous, uneasy, and dejected, and suddenly begins to hate the man who has taken advantage of her; and then, when her love is not understood or returned, she sinks into despondency, and becomes either a hater of

> He who knows how to make himself beloved by women becomes an object of their love.

mankind altogether or, hating her own man, she has recourse to other men."

On Creating Confidence in the Girl

On Courtship, and the Manifestations of the Feelings by Outward Signs and Deeds

poor man possessed of good qualities, a man born of a low family possessed of mediocre qualities, a neighbor possessed of wealth, and one under the control of his father, mother, or brothers, should not marry without endeavoring to gain over the girl from her childhood to love and esteem them. Thus a boy separated from his parents, and living in the house of his uncle, should try to gain over the daughter of his uncle, or some other girl, even though she be previously betrothed to another. And this

way of gaining over a girl, says
Ghotakamukha, is unexceptionable,
because Dharma can be accomplished
by means of it, as well as by any
other way of marriage.

When a boy has thus begun to woo
the girl he loves, he should spend
his time with her and amuse her
with various games and diversions
fitted for their age and acquaintance-
ship, such as picking and collecting
flowers, making garlands of flowers,
playing the parts of members of a
fictitious family, cooking food, playing
with dice, playing with cards,
the game of odd and even, the game
of finding out the middle finger, the
game of six pebbles, and such other
games as may be prevalent in the
country, and agreeable to the disposition of the girl. In addition to this,
he should carry on various amusing

When a boy has thus begun to woo the girl he loves, he should spend his time with her and amuse her with various games and diversions.

games played by several persons
together, such as hide-and-seek, playing with seeds, hiding things in several small heaps of wheat and looking
for them, blind-man's buff, gymnastic
exercises, and other games of the
same sort in company with the girl,
her friends, and female attendants.
The man should also show great
kindness to any woman whom the
girl thinks fit to be trusted, and
should also make new acquaintances,
but above all he should attach to himself by kindness and little services the
daughter of the girl's nurse, for if she
be gained over, even though she
comes to know of his design, she does
not cause any obstruction, but is
sometimes even able to effect a union
between him and the girl. And
though she knows the true character
of the man, she always talks of his
many excellent qualities to the parents

and relations of the girl, even though she may not be desired to do so by him.

In this way the man should do whatever the girl takes most delight in, and he should get for her whatever she may have a desire to possess. Thus he should procure for her such playthings as may be hardly known to other girls. He may also show her a ball dyed with various colors, and other curiosities of the same sort; and should give her dolls made of cloth, wood, buffalo horn, ivory, wax, flour, or earth; also utensils for cooking food; and figures in wood, such as a man and woman standing, a pair of rams or goats or sheep; also temples made of earth,

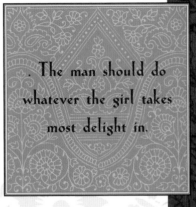

. The man should do whatever the girl takes most delight in.

On Courtship, and the Manifestations of the Feelings by Outward Signs and Deeds

bamboo, or wood, dedicated to various goddesses, and cages for parrots, cuckoos, starlings, quails, cocks, and partridges; water vessels of different sorts and of elegant forms, machines for throwing water about, guitars, stands for putting images upon, stools, lac, red arsenic, yellow ointment, vermilion and collyrium, as well as sandalwood, saffron, betel nut and betel leaves. Such things should be given at different times whenever he gets a good opportunity of meeting her in public, according to circumstances. In short, he should try in every way to make her look upon him as one who would do for her everything that she wanted to be done.

In the next place he should get her to meet him in some place privately, and should then tell her that the reason for his giving presents to her in secret was the fear that the parents of both of them might be displeased, and then he may add that the things which he had given her had been much desired by other people. When her love begins to show signs of increasing, he should relate to her agreeable stories if she expresses a wish to hear such narratives. Or if she takes delight in legerdemain, he should amaze her by performing various tricks of jugglery; or if she feels a great curiosity to see a performance of the various arts, he should show his own skill in them. When she is delighted with singing, he should entertain her with music, and on certain days, and at the time of going together to moonlight fairs and festivals, and at the time of her return after being absent from home, he should present her with bouquets of flowers and with chaplets for the

On Courtship, and the Manifestations of the Feelings by Outward Signs and Deeds

head and with ear ornaments and rings, for these are the proper occasions on which such things should be presented.

He should also teach the daughter of the girl's nurse all the sixty-four means of pleasure practiced by men, and under this pretext should also inform her of his great skill in the art of sexual enjoyment. All this time he should wear a fine dress, and make as good an appearance as possible, for young women love men who live with them, and who are handsome, good looking, and well dressed. As for the saying that though women may fall in love, they still make no effort themselves to gain over the object of their affections, that is only a matter of idle talk.

Now, a girl always shows her love by

outward signs and actions such as the following: She never looks the man in the face, and becomes abashed when she is looked at by him; under some pretext or other she shows her limbs to him; she looks secretly at him, though he has gone away from her side; hangs down her head when she is asked some question by him, and answers in indistinct words and unfinished sentences, delights to be in his company for a long time, speaks to her attendants in a peculiar tone with the hope of attracting his attention toward her when she is at a distance from him, and does not wish to go from the place where he is; under some pretext or other she makes him look at

All this time he should wear a fine dress, and make as good an appearance as possible.

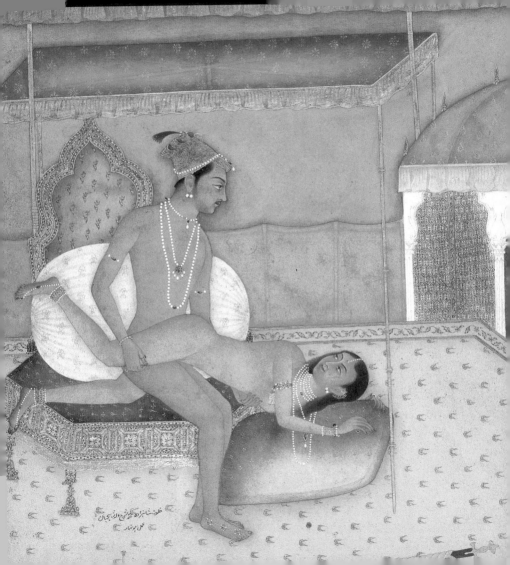

different things, narrates to him tales
and stories very slowly so that she
may continue conversing with him
for a long time; kisses and embraces
before him a child sitting in her lap;
draws ornamental marks on the
foreheads of her female servants, per-
forms sportive and graceful movements when her attendants speak
jestingly to her in the presence of
her lover; confides in her lover's
friends, and respects and obeys them;
shows kindness to his servants, con-
verses with them and engages them
to do her work as if she were their
mistress, and listens attentively to
them when they tell stories about
her lover to somebody else; enters
his house when induced to do so by
the daughter of her nurse, and by her
assistance manages to converse and
play with him; avoids being seen by
her lover when she is not dressed and

decorated; gives him by the hand of her female friend her ear ornament, ring, or garland of flowers that he may have asked to see; always wears anything that he may have presented to her, becomes dejected when any other bridegroom is mentioned by her parents, and does not mix with those who may be of his party, or who may support his claims.

> "A man who has seen and perceived the feeling of the girl toward him.... should do everything in his power to effect a union with her."

There are also some verses on the subject, as follows:

"A man who has seen and perceived the feelings of the girl toward him, and who has noticed the outward signs and movements by which those feelings are expressed, should

do everything in his power to effect
a union with her. He should gain
over a young girl by childlike sports;
a damsel come of age by his skill in
the arts, and a girl that loves him, by
having recourse to persons in whom
she confides."

On Courtship, and the Manifestations of the Feelings
by Outward Signs and Deeds

ON THINGS TO BE DONE ONLY
BY THE MAN, AND THE ACQUISITION
OF THE GIRL THEREBY.
ALSO, WHAT IS TO BE DONE BY
A GIRL TO GAIN OVER A MAN,
AND SUBJECT HIM TO HER

ow, when the girl begins to show her love by outward signs and motions, as described in the last chapter, the lover should try to gain her over entirely by various ways and means, such as the following:

When engaged with her in any game or sport, he should intentionally hold her hand. He should practice upon her the various kinds of embraces, such as the touching embrace, and others already described in a preceding chapter. He should show her a pair of human beings cut out of the

*On Things to Be Done Only by the Man,
and the Acquistion of the Girl Thereby*

leaf of a tree, and suchlike things, at intervals. When engaged in water sports, he should dive at a distance from her, and come up close to her. He should show an increased liking for the new foliage of the trees and suchlike things. He should describe to her the pangs he suffers on her account. He should relate to her the beautiful dream that he has had with reference to other women. At parties and assemblies of his caste he should sit near her, and touch her under some pretense or other, and having placed his foot upon hers, he should slowly touch each of her toes, and press the ends of the nails; if successful in this, he should get hold of her foot with his hand and repeat the same thing. He should also press a finger of her hand between his toes when she happens to be washing his feet; and whenever he gives anything

When the girl begins
to show her love by
outward signs and
motions, the lover
should try to gain
over entirely by
various ways
and means.

to her or takes anything from her, he should show her by his manner and looks how much he loves her.

He should sprinkle upon her the water brought for rinsing his mouth; and when alone with her in a lonely place, or in darkness, he should make love to her, and tell her the true state of his mind without distressing her in any way.

Whenever he sits with her on the same seat or bed he should say to her, "I have something to tell you in private," and then, when she comes to hear it in a quiet place, he should express his love to her more by manner and signs than by words. When he comes to know the state of her feelings toward him, he should pretend to be ill, and should make her come to his house to speak to him.

There he should intentionally hold her hand and place it on his eyes and forehead, and under the pretense of preparing some medicine for him he should ask her to do the work for his sake in the following words: "This work must be done by you, and by nobody else." When she wants to go away he should let her go, with an earnest request to come and see him again. This device of illness should be continued for three days and three nights. After this, when she begins coming to see him frequently, he should carry on long conversations with her, for, says Ghotakamukha, "though a man loves a girl ever so much, he never succeeds in winning her without a great deal of

> When alone with her in a lonely place, or in darkness, he should make love to her.

On Things to Be Done Only by the Man, and the Acquistion of the Girl Thereby

talking." At last, when the man finds the girl completely won over, he may then begin to enjoy her. As for the saying that women grow less timid than usual during the evening, at night, and in darkness, and are desirous of congress at those times, and do not oppose men then, and should only be enjoyed at these hours, it is a matter of talk only.

When it is impossible for the man to carry on his endeavors alone, he should, by means of the daughter of her nurse, or of a female friend in whom she confides, cause the girl to be brought to him without making known to her his design, and he should then proceed with her in the manner above described. Or he should in the beginning send his own female servant to live with the girl as her friend, and should then gain her over by her means.

At last, when he knows the state of her feeling by her outward manner and conduct toward him at religious ceremonies, marriage ceremonies, fairs, festivals, theaters, public assemblies, and suchlike occasions, he should begin to enjoy her when she is alone, for Vatsyayana lays it down that women, when resorted to at proper times and in proper places, do not turn away from their lovers.

When a girl, possessed of good qualities and well bred, though born of a humble family, or destitute of wealth, and not therefore desired by her equals, or an orphan girl, or one deprived of her parents, but observing the rules of her family and caste, wishes to bring about her own marriage when she comes of age, such a

*On Things to Be Done Only by the Man,
and the Acquistion of the Girl Thereby*

girl should endeavor to gain over a strong and good-looking young man or a person whom she thinks would marry her on account of the weakness of his mind, and even without the consent of his parents. She should do this by such means as would endear her to the said person, as well as by frequently seeing and meeting him. Her mother also should constantly cause them to meet by means of her female friends, and the daughter of her nurse. The girl herself should try to get alone with her beloved in some quiet place, and at odd times should give him flowers, betel nut, betel leaves, and perfumes. She should also show her skill in the practice of the arts, in

Although the girl loves the man, she should not offer herself, or make the first overtures.

shampooing, in scratching and in pressing with the nails. She should also talk to him on the subjects he likes best, and discuss with him the ways and means of gaining over and winning the affections of a girl.

But old authors say that although the girl loves the man ever so much, she should not offer herself, or make the first overtures, for a girl who does this loses her dignity, and is liable to be scorned and rejected. But when the man shows his wish to enjoy her, she should be favorable to him, and should show no change in her demeanor when he embraces her, and should receive all the manifestations of his love as if she were ignorant of the state of his mind. But when he tries to kiss her she should oppose him; when he begs to be allowed to have sexual intercourse with her she

On Things to Be Done Only by the Man,
and the Acquistion of the Girl Thereby

"A girl who is much sought after should marry the man she likes, and whom she thinks would be obedient to her, and capable of giving her pleasure."

should let him touch her private parts
only and with considerable difficulty;
and though importuned by him, she
should not yield herself up to him as
if of her own accord, but should resist
his attempts to have her. Moreover, it
is only when she is certain that she is
truly loved and that her lover is
indeed devoted to her, and will not
change his mind, that she should
then give herself up to him, and persuade him to marry her quickly. After
losing her virginity she should tell her
confidential friends about it.

Here ends discourse of the efforts of a
girl to gain over a man.

There are also some verses on the
subject, as follows:

"A girl who is much sought after
should marry the man she likes, and

whom she thinks would be obedient to her, and capable of giving her pleasure. But when from the desire of wealth a girl is married by her parents to a rich man without taking into consideration the character or looks of the bridegroom, or when given to a man who has several wives, she never becomes attached to the man, even though he be endowed with good qualities, obedient to her will, active, strong, and healthy, and anxious to please her in every way. A husband who is obedient but yet master of himself, though he be poor and not good looking, is better than one who is common to many women, even though he be handsome and attractive. The wives of rich men, where there are many wives, are not generally attached to their husbands, and are not confidential with them, and even though they possess all the external enjoyments of life, still have recourse to other men. A man who is of a low mind, who has fallen from his social position, and who is much given to traveling, does not deserve to be married; neither does one who has many wives and children, or one who is devoted to sport and gambling, and who comes to his wife only when he likes. Of all the lovers of a girl, he only is her true husband who possesses the qualities that are liked by her, and such a husband enjoys real superiority over her only because he is the husband of love."

ON THE MEANS OF ATTRACTING OTHERS TO YOURSELF

On Personal Adornment,
On Subjugating the Hearts of
Others, and on Tonic Medicines

hen a person fails to obtain the object of his desires by any of the ways previously related, he should then have recourse to other ways of attracting others to himself.

Now, good looks, qualities, youth, and liberality are the chief and most natural means of making a person agreeable in the eyes of others. But in the absence of these, a man or woman must have resort to artificial means, or to art, and the following are some recipes that may be found useful:

On Personal Adornment; On Subjugating the Hearts of Others; and on Tonic Medicines

a   An ointment made of the *Tabernaemontana coronaria*, the *Costus speciosus* or arabicus, and the *Flacourtia Cataphracta*, can be used as an unguent of adornment.

b   If a fine powder is made of the above plants, and applied to the wick of a lamp, which is made to burn with the oil of blue vitriol, the black pigment or lampblack produced therefrom, when applied to the eyelashes, has the effect of making a person look lovely.

c   The oil of the hogweed, the *Echites putescens*, the sarina plant, the yellow amaranth, and the leaf of the nymphae, if applied to the body, has the same effect.

d   A black pigment from the same plants produces a similar effect.

When a person fails to obtain the object of his desires by any of the ways previously related, he should then have recourse to other ways of attracting others to himself.

e   By eating the powder of the *Nelumbium speciosum*, the blue lotus, and the *Mesna roxburghii*, with ghee and honey, a man becomes lovely in the eyes of others.

f   The above things, together with the *Tabernaemontana coronaria*, and the *Xanthochymus pictorius*, if used as ointment, produce the same results.

g   If the bone of a peacock or of a hyena be covered with gold, and tied on the right hand, it makes a man lovely in the eyes of other people.

h   In the same way, if a bead, made of the seed of the jujube, or of the conch shell, be enchanted by the incantations of those well skilled in the science of magic, and tied on the hand, it produces the same results as described above.

i   When a female attendant arrives at the

age of puberty, her master should keep her secluded, and when men ardently desire her because of her seclusion, and because of the difficulty of approaching her, he should then bestow her hand on such a person as may endow her with wealth and happiness.

This is a means of increasing the loveliness of a person in the eyes of others.

In the same way, when the daughter of a courtesan arrives at the age of puberty, the mother should get together a lot of young men of the same age, disposition, and knowledge as her daughter, and tell them that she would give her in marriage to the person who would give her presents of a particular kind.

After this, the daughter should be kept in seclusion as far as possible, and the mother should give her in marriage to the man who may be ready to give her presents agreed upon. If the mother is unable to get so much out of the man, she should show some of her own things as having been given to the daughter by the bridegroom.

Or the mother may allow her daughter to be married to the man privately, as if she were ignorant of the whole affair, and then, pretending that it has come to her knowledge, she may give her consent to the union.

The daughter, too, should make herself attractive to the sons of wealthy citizens, unknown to her mother, and make them attached to her, and for this purpose should meet them at the time of learning to sing, and in places where music is played, and at the houses of other people, and then request her mother, through a female friend or servant, to be allowed to unite herself to the man who is most agreeable to her.[1]

When the daughter of a courtesan is thus given to a man, the ties of marriage should be observed for one year, and after that she may do what she likes. But even after the end of the year, when otherwise engaged, if she should be now and then invited by her first husband to come and see him, she should put aside her present gain, and go to him for the night.

Such is the mode of temporary marriage among courtesans, and of increasing their loveliness and their value in the eyes of others. What has been said about them should also be understood to apply to the daughters of dancing women, whose mothers should give them only to such persons as are likely to become useful to them in various ways.

It was a custom of the courtesans of Oriental countries to give their daughters temporarily in marriage when they come of age, and after they have received an education in the *Kama Sutra* and other arts.

On Personal Adornment; On Subjugating the Hearts of Others; and on Tonic Medicines

Thus ends discourse of the ways of making oneself lovely in the eyes of others.

a   If a man, after anointing his lingam with a mixture of the powders of the white thorn apple, the long pepper and the black pepper, and honey, engages in sexual union with a woman, he makes her subject to his will.

b   The application of a mixture of the leaf of the plant vatodbhranta, of the flowers thrown on a human corpse when carried out to be burned, and of the powder of the bones of the peacock, and of the jiwanjiva bird produces the same effect.

c   The remains of a kite who has died a natural death, ground into powder, and mixed with cowhage and honey, has also the same effect.

d   Anointing oneself with an ointment

made of the plant *Emblica myrobolans* has the power of subjecting women to one's will.

e   If a man cuts into small pieces the sprouts of the vajnasunhi plant, and dips them into a mixture of red arsenic and sulphur, and then dries them seven times, and applies this powder mixed with honey to his lingam, he can subjugate a woman to his will directly he has had sexual union with her; or if by burning these very sprouts at night and looking at the smoke, he sees a golden moon behind, he will then be successful with any woman; or if he throws some of the powder of these same sprouts mixed with the excrement of a monkey upon a maiden, she will not be given in marriage to anybody else.

f   If pieces of the orrisroot are dressed with

Anointing oneself
with an ointment
made of the plant
Emblica myrobolans
has the power of
subjecting women
to one's will.

the oil of the mango, and placed for six months in a hole made in the trunk of the sisu tree, and are then taken out and made up into an ointment, and applied to the lingam, this is said to serve as the means of subjugating women.

G If a bone of a camel is dipped into the juice of the plant *Eclipta prostata*, and then burned, and the black pigment produced from its ashes is placed in a box also made of the bone of a camel, and applied together with antimony to the eyelashes with a pencil also made of the bone of a camel, then that pigment is said to be very pure, and wholesome for the eyes, and serves as a means of subjugating others to the person who uses it. The same effect can be produced by black pigment made of the bones of hawks, vultures, and peacocks.

Thus ends discourse of the ways of subjugating others to one's own will.

Now, the means of increasing sexual vigor are as follows:

a A man obtains sexual vigor by drinking milk mixed with sugar, the root of the uchchata plant, the pipar chaba, and licorice.

b Drinking milk mixed with sugar, and having the testicle of a ram or goat boiled in it, is also productive of vigor.

c The drinking of the juice of the *Hedysarum gangeticum*, the kuili, and the kshirika plant, mixed with milk, produces the same effect.

ᴆ The seed of long pepper, along with the seeds of the *Sansevieria roxburghiana*, and the *Hedysarum gangeticum* plant, all pounded together, and mixed with milk, is productive of a similar result.

e   According to ancient authors, if a man pounds the seeds or roots of the *Trapa bispinosa*, the kasurika, the tuscan jasmine, and licorice, together with the kshirikapoli (a kind of onion), and puts the powder into milk mixed with sugar and ghee, and having boiled the whole mixture on a moderate fire, drinks the paste so formed, he will be able to enjoy innumerable women.

f   In the same way, if a man mixes rice with the eggs of the sparrow, and having boiled this in milk, adds to it ghee and honey, and drinks as much of it as is necessary, this will produce the same effect.

On Personal Adornment; On Subjugating the Hearts of Others; and on Tonic Medicines

G   If a man takes the outer covering of sesame seeds, and soaks them with the eggs of sparrows, and then, having boiled them in milk, mixed with sugar and ghee, along with the fruits of the *Trapa bispinosa* and the kasurika plant, and adds to it the flour of wheat and beans, and then drinks this composition, he is said to be able to enjoy many women.

ḥ   If ghee, honey, sugar, and licorice in equal quantities, the juice of the fennel plant, and milk are mixed together, this nectar-like composition is said to be holy, and provocative of sexual vigor, a preservative of life, and sweet to the taste.

i   The drinking of a paste composed of the *Asparagus racemosus*, the shvadaushtra plant, the guduchi plant, the long pepper, and licorice, boiled in milk, honey, and ghee, in the spring, is said to have the same effect as the above.

j Boiling the *Asparagus racemosus* and the shvadaushtra plant, along with the pounded fruits of the *Premna spinosa* in water, and drinking the same, is said to act in the same way.

k Drinking boiled ghee, or clarified butter, in the morning, during the spring season, is said to be beneficial to health and strength, and agreeable to the taste.

l If the powder of the seed of the shvadaushtra plant and the flour of barley are mixed together in equal parts, and a portion of it, two palas in weight, is eaten every morning on getting up, it has the same effect at the preceding recipe.

There are also verses on the subject, as follows:

"The means[2] of producing love and sexual vigor should be learned from the science of medicine, from the Vedas, from those who are learned in the arts of magic, and from confidential relatives. No means should be tried which are doubtful in their effects, which are likely to cause injury to the body, which involve the death of animals, or which bring us in contact with impure things. Only such means should be used as are holy, acknowledged to be good, and approved of by Brahmans and friends."

2 From the earliest times Oriental authors have concerned themselves with aphrodisiacs. The following note on the subject is taken from page 29 of a translation of the Hindu *Art of Love*, otherwise the *Ananga Ranga*: "Most Eastern treatises divide aphrodisiacs into two different kinds: (1) the mechanical or natural, such as scarification, flagellation, etc.; and (2) the medicinal or artificial. To the former belong the application of insects, as is practiced by some savage races; and all Orientalists will remember the tale of the old Brahman whose young wife insisted upon his being again stung by a wasp."

The means of
producing love and
sexual vigor should
be learned from the
science of medicine,
from the Vedas, from
those who are
learned in the arts of
magic, and from
confidential relatives.

On the Ways of Exciting Desire, and on Miscellaneous Experiments and Recipes

f a man is unable to satisfy a Hastini, or elephant woman, he should have recourse to various means to excite her passion. At the commencement he should run her yoni with his hand or fingers, and not begin to have intercourse with her until she becomes excited, or experiences pleasure. This is one way of exciting a woman.

Or he may make use of certain Apadravyas, or things which are put on or around the lingam to supplement its length or its thickness, so as

On the Ways of Exciting Desire;
and on Miscellaneous Experiments and Recipes

to fit it to the yoni. In the opinion of Babhravya, these Apadravyas should be made of gold, silver, copper, iron, ivory, buffalo's horn, various kinds of wood, tin, or lead, and should be soft, cool, provocative of sexual vigor, and well fitted to serve the intended pur-pose. Vatsyayana, however, says that they may be made according to the natural liking of each individual.

The following are the different kinds of Apadravyas:

1. "The armlet" (Valaya) should be of the same size as the lingam, and should have its outer surface made rough with globules.

2. "The couple" (Sanghati) is formed of two armlets.

3. "The bracelet" (Chudaka) is made by

joining three or more armlets, until they come up to the required length of the lingam.

4   "The single bracelet" is formed by wrapping a single wire around the lingam, according to its dimensions.

5   The Kantuka or Jalaka is a tube open at both ends, with a hole through it, outwardly rough and studded with soft globules, and made to fit the size of the yoni, and tied to the waist.

When such a thing cannot be obtained, then a tube made of the wood apple, or tubular stalk of the bottle gourd, or a reed made soft with oil and extracts of plants, and tied to the waist with string, may be made use of, as well as a row of soft pieces of wood tied together.

The above are the things that can be

used in connection with, or in place of, the lingam.

The people of the southern countries think that true sexual pleasure cannot be obtained without perforating the lingam, and they therefore cause it to be pierced like the lobes of the ears of an infant pierced for earrings.

> He may make use of certain things which are put on or around the lingam to supplement its length or its thickness.

Now, when a young man perforates his lingam he should pierce it with a sharp instrument, and then stand in water as long as the blood continues to flow. At night he should engage in sexual intercourse, even with vigor, so as to clean the hole. After this he should continue to wash the hole with

On the Ways of Exciting Desire;
and on Miscellaneous Experiments and Recipes

decoctions, and increase the size by putting into it small pieces of cane, and the *Wrightea antidysenterica*, thus gradually enlarging the orifice. It may also be washed with licorice mixed with honey, and the size of the hole increased by the fruit stalks of the simapatra plant. The hole should also be anointed with a small quantity of oil.

In the hole made in the lingam a man may put Apadravyas of various forms, such as the "round," the "round on one side," the "wooden mortar," the "flower," the "armlet," the "bone of the heron," the "goad of the elephant," the "collection of eight balls," the "lock of hair," the "place where four roads meet," and other things named according to their forms and means of using them. All these Apadravyas should be rough on the outside according to their requirements.

The ways of enlarging the lingam must now be related.

When a man wishes to enlarge his lingam, he should rub it with the bristles of certain insects that live in trees, and then, after rubbing it for ten nights with oils, he should again rub it with the bristles as before. By continuing to do this a swelling will gradually be produced in the lingam, and he should then lie on a cot, and cause his lingam to hang down through a hole in the cot. After this, he should take away all the pain from the swelling by using cool concoctions. The swelling, which is called "Suka," and is often brought about among the people of the Dravidian country, lasts for life.

If the lingam is rubbed with the following things, namely, the plant

Physalis flexuosa, the shavara-kandaka plant, the jalasuka plant, the fruit of the eggplant, the butter of a she-buffalo, the hasti-charma plant, and the juice of the vajrarasna plant, a swelling lasting for one month will be produced.

By rubbing it with oil boiled in the concoctions of the above things, the same effect will be produced, but lasting for six months.

The enlargement of the lingam is also effected by rubbing it or moistening it with oil boiled in the concoctions of the above things, the same effect will be produced, but lasting for six months.

The enlargement of the lingam is also effected by rubbing it or moistening it with oil boiled on a moderate fire along with the seeds of the pomegranate, and the cucumber, the juices of the valuka plant, the hasti-charma plant, and the eggplant.

In addition to the above, other means may be learned from experience and confidential persons.

The miscellaneous experiments and recipes are as follows:

a If a man mixes the powder of the milk hedge plant and the kantaka plant with the excrement of a monkey and the powdered root of the lanjalika plant, and throws this mixture on a woman, she will not love anybody else afterward.

b If a man thickens the juice of the fruits of the *Cassia fistula* and the *Eugenia jambolana* by mixing them with the powder of the soma plant, the *Vernonia anthelmintica*, the *Eclipta prostata*, and the lohopa-jihirka, and applies this

At the COMMENCEMENT he should RUN her yoni with his hand or fingers, and not begin to have intercourse with her until she becomes excited, or experiences pleasure.

278

composition to the yoni of a woman,
and then has sexual intercourse with
her, his love for her will be destroyed.

ᴄ The same effect is produced if a man
has connection with a woman who
has bathed in the buttermilk of a she-
buffalo mixed with the powders of
gopalika plant, the banupadika plant,
and the yellow amaranth.

ᴆ An ointment made of the flowers of
the *Nauclea cadamba*, the hog plum,
and the *Eugenia jambolana*, and used
by a woman, causes her to be disliked
by her husband.

ᴇ Garlands made of the above flowers,
when worn by the woman, produce
the same effect.

ꜰ An ointment made of the fruit of the
Asteracantha longifolia (kokilaksha) will

*On the Ways of Exciting Desire;
and on Miscellaneous Experiments and Recipes*

contract the yoni of a Hastini, or elephant woman, and this contraction lasts for one night.

G An ointment made by pounding the roots of the *Nelumbium speciosum* and of the blue lotus, and the powder of the plant *Physalis flexuosa* mixed with ghee and honey, will enlarge the yoni of the Mrigi, or deer woman.

ħ An ointment made of the fruit of the *Emblica myrobolans*, soaked in the milky juice of the milk hedge plant, of the soma plant, the *Calotropis gigantea*, and the juice of the fruit of the *Vernonia anthelmintica*, will make the hair white.

ɪ The juice of the roots of the madayantika plant, the yellow amaranth, the anjanika plant, the *Clitoria ternatea*, and the shlakshnaparni plant, used as a lotion, will make the hair grow.

j   An ointment made by boiling the above roots in oil, and rubbed in, will make the hair black, and will also gradually restore hair that has fallen off.

k   If lac is saturated seven times in the sweat of the testicle of a white horse, and applied to a red lip, the lip will become white.

l   The color of the lips can be regained by means of the madayantika and other plants mentioned above under **i**.

M   A woman who hears a man playing on a reed pipe which has been dressed with the juices of the bahupadika plant, the *Tabernaemontana coronaria*, the *Costus speciosus* or arabicus, the *Pinus deodora*, the *Euphorbia antiquorum*, the vajra and the kantaka plant, becomes his slave.

On the Ways of Exciting Desire;
and on Miscellaneous Experiments and Recipes

N If food be mixed with the fruit of the thorn apple (datura), it causes intoxication.

O If water be mixed with oil and the ashes of any kind of grass except the kusha grass, it becomes the color of milk.

P If yellow myrobolans, the hog plum, the shrawana plant, and the priyangu plant be all pounded together, and applied to iron pots, these pots become red.

Q If a lamp, trimmed with oil extracted from the shrawana and priyangu plants (its wick being made of cloth and the slough of the skins of snakes), is lighted, and long pieces of wood placed near it, those pieces of wood will resemble so many snakes.

R Drinking the milk of a white cow who has a white calf at her foot is

auspicious, produces fame, and preserves life.

s The blessings of venerable Brahmans,
well propitiated, have the same effect.

There are also some verses in conclusion:

"Thus I have written in a few words
these *Aphorisms on Love*, after reading
the texts of ancient authors, and following the ways of enjoyment mentioned in them.

"He who is acquainted with the true
principles of this science pays regard
to Dharma, Artha, Kama, and to his
own experiences, as well as to the
teachings of others, and does not act
simply on the dictates of his own
desire. As for the errors in the science
of love which I have mentioned in
this work, on my own authority as an

On the Ways of Exciting Desire;
and on Miscellaneous Experiments and Recipes

author, I have, immediately after mentioning them, carefully censured and prohibited them.

"An act is never looked upon with indulgence for the simple reason that it is authorized by the science, because it ought to be remembered that it is the intention of the science that the rules which it contains should be acted upon only in particular cases. After reading and considering the works of Babhravya and other ancient authors, and thinking over the meaning of the rules given by them, the *Kama Sutra* was composed, according to the precepts of Holy Writ, for the benefit of the world, by Vatsyayana, while leading the life of a religious student, and wholly engaged in the contemplation of the Deity.

"This work is not intended to be used

"A person acquainted with the true principles of this science, and who preserves his Dharma, Artha, and Kama... is sure to obtain mastery over his senses."

> "An intelligent and prudent person, attending to Dharma and Artha, and attending to Kama also, obtains success in everything."

merely as an instrument for satisfying our desires. A person acquainted with the true principles of this science, and who preserves his Dharma, Artha, and Kama, and has regard for the practices of the people, is sure to obtain the mastery over his senses.

"In short, an intelligent and prudent person, attending to Dharma and Artha, and attending to Kama also, without becoming the slave of his passions, obtains success in everything that he may undertake."

287

On the Ways of Exciting Desire;
and on Miscellaneous Experiments and Recipes